Strangers to Failure

Developing Faith and Power in an Awesome God

by
Benson Idahosa

Harrison House
Tulsa, Oklahoma

2nd Printing
Over 12,500 in Print

Strangers to Failure —
Developing Faith and Power in an Awesome God
ISBN 089274-761-7
Copyright © 1993 by Archbishop Benson A. Idahosa
P. O. Box 29400
Washington, D. C. 20017

Published by Harrison House, Inc.
P. O. Box 35035
Tulsa, Oklahoma 74153

Dedication

This book is dedicated to all who are seeking new life in faith for victorious living. It comes to build you, strengthen you, and spur you on to new heights; above all, to lift you up to the standard God wants you to reach.

It is dedicated especially to my dear wife and family who have stood by me in all our "zero hours."

Behold a blessing in your hands!

Contents

Author's Preface:
The Faith Factor

A prominent Bible scholar once said: "Take from a man his wealth and you hinder him; take from him his faith and hope and you stop him." The Bible says that without faith it is impossible to please God. (Heb. 11:6.) In fact, without faith you cannot walk with God. If you cannot please God without faith, then please Him by your faith in Him and in His Word.

To believe that there is a Supreme Being Who created heaven and earth is one thing. To believe and place confidence in Him to rule and reign in your life is another issue. That is where your faith comes in. The answer to facing the trials and tribulations of life lies in trusting God to bring you through them to life's highest point. Faith is the active force which draws the thin line between success and failure. Faith in God through Christ declares, "The Lord will bring me to a successful end." (Josh. 1:8; Jer. 29:11.)

A great man once said, "What you have undeveloped in you has no value." This book will show you how I placed value on my faith, and by so doing was able to face and triumph over the "zero hours" in my life. Faith in God changed my destiny — and that of millions of people with whom I have shared that faith around the world.

I say to you, "Arise in your faith; use it in *your* zero hours." I have placed in your hands the secret to happy, abundant, and successful life. This secret worked for me. God can make it work for you too.

Have faith in God!

Archbishop Benson A. Idahosa
Benin City, Nigeria

1

Facing Reality With Faith

Let us then approach the throne of grace with confidence, so that we may receive mercy and find grace to help us in our time of need.

Hebrews 4:16 NIV

All power has a source, and a born-again Christian should be absolutely certain of where his power comes from. The knowledge that God's power is fully available to you will, in one way or another, calm the waves in your life when stormy days arrive.

I speak from experience: the realization that the unseen hand of God controls my life brought me to a turning point. In this book, I will tell you about the difference this realization has made in my walk with the Lord. I will also describe to you how other servants of the Lord surmounted the trials, tribulations, temptations, and turbulence that stood in their way. They overcame, I have overcome, and so will you — today!

Zero hours come upon everyone at one time or another — usually with the suddenness of Job's misfortunes. What are "zero hours"? Zero hours are those bleak times, the lean seasons, the occasions in life when things come to a dead end. Suddenly there is no light at the end of the tunnel, and everything seems upside down. In the agony and deep desperation of such times, some can only shout in hopelessness, "I am ruined; I am finished!"

If that is the situation in which you find yourself right now, hold on, my friend! It is not the end. No believer in Jesus Christ ever needs to cry out that all is lost, that there is no hope. You will soon know why I make this bold statement.

How can you "turn the tables" on the devil? How do you brace yourself to deal courageously with the zero hours which you will face in life, putting them behind you in victory? Many people have asked, "How do I acquire the power to stand fast when the inevitable zero hours come upon me?" That is a good question. It is time every born-again Christian realized that the purpose of Christianity is not to teach us believers how to avoid or eliminate difficulty, but to nurture within us the strength of character necessary to offset difficulty when it comes. Christianity does not make life easy, rather it provides the strength needed to face and overcome the trials of life.

Christianity does not remove the red lights, stumps, setbacks, and tragedies of life. But we have good reason to believe that our walk with God in Christ gives us vital armor and a tough skin as protection when the zero hour sneaks in. The mature person has the cool-headedness and stability to remain calm and collected, being anxious for nothing. (Phil. 4:6). Yet many people fret and panic when they encounter hardship. There is truth in the old statement that "when the going gets tough, the tough get going."

The generalization of issues and a collective prescription of solutions to individual problems of life have always proved a gamble that does not pay off. The only remedy for a crisis situation in the Christian walk lies in the Word of God, for heaven and earth will pass away, but God's Word will never pass away. (Matt. 24:35.)

Your zero hours should not find you unprepared. But whether they do or not depends a great deal upon whether you know the source of your power. As you read this book, I pray that the Father of glory will give you the Spirit of wisdom and revelation as you walk in victory through Christ. Most of all, I pray that the eyes of your understanding be enlightened (Eph. 1:17,18), that you may know the power in the name of Jesus and His blood shed at Calvary. (Mark 16:17,18; 1 Pet. 1:18,19; 1 John 1:7; Rev. 12:11.)

Facing the Zero Hours

Every passing minute is a matter of life and death for someone torn by the conflicts of a difficult situation. Satan keeps knocking at every door, breaking windows to try to get in. Can you stand against the onslaught? As you read these words, somewhere a family is on the brink of a problem or disaster or sudden change in affairs which will have serious repercussions in their marriage, children, and friends. Although many people fumble in the darkness, overcome by the circumstances of life, we Christians can be assured that every problem we encounter contains the seed of God's solution. Has the Lord not said, **Call unto me, and I will answer thee, and shew thee great and mighty things, which thou knowest not** (Jer. 33:3)?

As a minister of the gospel of salvation and deliverance, it is agonizing for me to see thousands of people — even many devout Christians — resigning themselves to their "fate." I know that through the blood of Jesus there is power to overcome sickness, disease, poverty, and all the other problems which beset so many in our world today.

Let's face facts. Do you know what it is to come face to face with abject poverty and to live at a bare subsistence level? Do you know how it feels to see your only child taken sick and to have no money to pay for a doctor or medicine? Have you ever felt the anguish of accumulating bills, when all means of settlement seem remote?

You may be a student and as yet relatively untouched by the complex problems which beset married couples and families today. But perhaps you still have had your fair share of the zero hours that life deals out to everyone.

I remember a conversation I had with a final-year university student as I went to preach on his campus. As I descended the stairs, I heard the clatter of feet behind me and what sounded like tearful shouts for attention. I swiveled around and immediately came face to face with a well-dressed, neat-looking young man.

"Please, Dr. Idahosa," he said, gasping for breath, a worried expression wrinkling his face, "I need help; I am in a fix."

"Calm down," I said, as he took his place by my side to recount his problem.

"Please, sir, this is my final year," he blurted out. "I have already failed once due to sudden illness and the exam I am taking tomorrow is my last chance. If I miss it," he stressed with a clenched fist, "I will have to give up."

A curtain of anxiety and uncertainty shrouded his tense face as he gazed upwardly, eagerly waiting for my reply. I took his hand firmly in mine and looked him in the eyes.

"Go in the peace of the Lord," I told him. "Victory and success are surely yours. Amen."

Zero hours such as the one faced by this young man sweep across our path without warning. All of a sudden, this graduating senior seemed to have his entire future threatened. This was his zero hour, and he needed divine intervention to help him face and meet the challenge.

Some of us have survived the extremities of a zero hour, and I believe we can show others the way to victory.

Some years ago, a tragic and unexpected incident struck my family. I share this testimony to the glory of God, in Whose hands my faith will always stand. I have often had to refrain from telling this story, but it brings my point into sharp focus and reveals what happens when the pendulum suddenly swings towards loss, consternation, and tragedy.

When Tragedy Came, Faith Was There Too

It had been an uneventful night. My family had gone to bed hale and hearty: there was giggling and there were smiles as we prayed, and the joy of the Lord was our strength. (Neh. 8:10.) I said goodnight to my children; they waved back to me and banged shut their doors. This is often the sort of peaceful atmosphere which the wicked one attempts to overthrow. But God is on our side, and He will scatter the enemy in our presence.

The next morning as I looked out over the balcony, the Word of God weaved through my mind: "This is the day the Lord has made; let us rejoice and be glad in it." (Ps. 118:24 NIV.) The dewy darkness was dispersing, and I listened to the melodious singing of the early morning birds. It was time for my family and me to prepare for our daily devotions.

As my wife walked a little distance ahead of me, I noticed what seemed to me a slight miscalculation in her step. Before I could even ask what the problem was, I saw her miss one more step and slump onto the carpet with a thud. There at my feet lay my dear wife, gasping for breath! There were no moments for guesswork or unnecessary questions! I knew that Satan was up to his tricks, and I refused to play games with him.

As cautiously as I could, I knelt down at Margaret's side, while the children looked on in confusion and fear. With considerable care, I took her drooping hand in mine. Then I noticed a sudden change come over her countenance: she blinked absent-mindedly. I said slowly, "Margaret, what is the matter; how do you feel?"

Repeatedly, I felt her pulse. Countless thoughts flashed through my mind. Believe me, if ever a husband needed to demonstrate strength, faith, and courage, I knew this was the hour. In the twinkling of an eye my wife's hand went limp and cold with sweat. I needed no medical expert to tell me that a gradual countdown had begun, and every minute counted for life or death. I decided according to God's unfailing and infallible Word not to take no for an answer.

The zero hour is, of course, full of fear. But it is also fraught with faith. You can pull through your zero hours if you stand firm on the solid rock which is Jesus Christ! His Word says confidently that in His name those Who believe in Him shall cast out devils and bring health to the sick and dying. (Mark 16:17.) I knew that I have authority over every scheme of Satan, and at that moment Isaiah 54:17, Malachi 3:11, Luke 10:19, Revelation 12:11, and a host of other scriptures flashed into my mind. I stood firm!

As I looked into the faces of my wife and children, tears filled my eyes. Margaret was *dead*! This could not be, no! But dead she was, stone dead. I called out to God; I cried out as never before. I sent the children back to their rooms to pray. With heavy feet and tear-soaked cheeks, they marched off. And there I knelt, all alone, beside my wife. She was suddenly lying dead in my arms. I did what I know to do best — I prayed. I stood before the throne of God and pleaded according to His Word, **Let us therefore come boldly unto the throne of grace, that we may obtain mercy, and find grace to help in time of need** (Heb. 4:16). I quoted this verse aloud to the Lord. I refused to give up. I pleaded with Him in the name of Jesus.

A glance at the alarm clock in my room told me that thirty minutes had passed. As much as I prayed, there was no sign of life in my wife. I began to perspire, but not to give up. The Word of God came forcefully to me, "Be still and see the salvation of the Lord." (2 Chron. 20:17.) I wondered how I could be still in such an hour. But I obeyed the Holy Spirit of God. I knew that He is in control and He is omniscient.

19

Then the Holy Spirit told me, "Breathe into her mouth, and she will come back to life." I acted immediately, without a moment's doubt, because I have implicit faith in the God I serve. In uplifted faith, I clasped my hands behind Margaret's neck and drew her up toward me. I breathed into her mouth. Immediately she opened her eyes, stared at my sweat-drained face, and clasped me firmly in a loving embrace. With a victorious shout of "Praise the Lord!" my children ran in to kiss their mother on both cheeks. I stood by and glorified the name of the living God! I had good reason to do so.

Dare to Believe

It is sad that we cannot foresee the zero hours that we will inevitably encounter at some time or another. But looking into the future is not my concern. The point I want you to understand is that you have total authority and immeasurable power based on God's Word to turn those cruel moments to your advantage. Would you allow God to do so as you place total faith in Him as I did? He has the almighty power and overflowing resources to transform every situation.

Dare to believe it, and God will perform a miracle for every setback along the way.

Where is the problem? In the family, at the office, in your marriage, business, study? We serve a God Whose hand surrounds and holds the answer to all our needs. God said to Jeremiah, **Behold, I am the Lord, the God of all flesh: is there any thing too hard for me?** (Jer. 32:27). God wants you to know that the hour of breakthrough has come at last. Arise and shine, for the light of God's power has come to lift every burden and affliction. God in His might and power will make those crooked paths straight, fill every valley, and bring every mountain low as you walk confidently with Him day by day.

The hour of liberation has come. It is time once more to lift high your head and *live!*

2
Faith Makes a Difference

...since we have been justified through faith, we have peace with God through our Lord Jesus Christ.

Romans 5:1 NIV

Faith in God is the most dynamic force known to mankind. And, as the Scriptures declare, faith comes by hearing the Word of God. (Rom. 10:17). It is now time to delve deep into the treasure of God's Word. Our purpose is to unearth timeless answers that will see you through the worst of your zero hours.

First, let's go to Colossians 1:10,11 (NIV) for a word of Scripture to unknot the mystery of *God's power* to deal with your problems:

And we pray this in order that you may live a life worthy of the Lord and may please him in every way....

being strengthened with all power according to his glorious might so that you may have great endurance and patience, and joy....

Here we see that God's power gives *endurance, patience,* and *joy.* The power that strengthens you eventually leads to joy.

The Key to Victory in Life

The key words here are *power, might, endurance, patience,* and *joy.* The Scriptures say specifically that you need power, God's power, to give you strength in your hour of need and fear. (2 Cor. 12:10, Eph. 6:10.) And

God backs up His power with His might. He can mobilize a host of angels, which (as we read in Hebrews 1:14) are **...ministering spirits, sent forth to minister for them who shall be heirs of salvation...,** which are the born-again Christians.

The Gospels show how God mobilized angels to minister to the Lord Jesus Christ after His temptation by Satan in the wilderness and also in the garden of Gethsemane. (Matt. 4:11; Luke 22:43.) God's might will also change circumstances on your behalf.

The next two key words are *endurance* and *patience*. It takes a good measure of both to survive the storms of life. (For further supporting scriptures on this subject read Romans 5:1-5 and James 1:2-4.) Patience will enable you to stand upon God's Word by faith, regardless of the severity of the situation you face.

Finally, there is always *joy* in God's deliverance, for which you have trusted by faith, and His joy is your strength! (Neh. 8:10.) Keep these simple truths in your heart.

Power for Your Zero Hour

All over the world, people react in similar ways to sudden crises. Some recoil into their shell and bemoan their fate; others just fizzle out and give up. Neither of these is God's answer to a sudden change in fortune.

What can be more agonizing, for example, than to work day and night for years to earn a college degree and then, after a pat on the back and a series of "well done" handshakes, to discover that you cannot get a job? No one can ever convince me that as a Kingdom child of the Most High God, that is all He has for you.

Scrap it from your thinking; it is the devil's lie. That *could* be your zero hour. But hold on!

Remember the words of the Apostle Paul who wrote, **Being confident of this very thing, that he which hath begun a good work in you will perform it until the day of Jesus Christ** (Phil. 1:6). This is God's standing promise to you — and, believe it, my friend, there *is* power for your zero hour.

Sometimes I come across people, even so-called believers (I don't know what they profess to believe), who hold that as children of God we should just take every circumstance, every negative development or disturbance of our peace, as what God has planned for us. Scripturally speaking, I cannot agree with that point of view. Jesus Christ boldly declared, **The thief** (Satan) **cometh not, but for to steal, and to kill, and to destroy...**(John 10:10). God offsets the works of the devil, as is shown in the second part of this well-known Scripture in which Jesus went on to proclaim, **...I am come that they might have life, and that they might have it more abundantly.** The devil can always do his worst to you, but God will surely do His best for you, giving you power for your zero hour.

Beloved, it is heartbreaking to hear negative, joy-killing confessions and testimonies from some believers. There is a great need of deliverance from such retrogressive, wrong thinking. Do you really think that God spent so much to redeem us just so we could then live in poverty and deprivation? That cannot be. We can trust God to transform our shortcomings and lead us to victory over our circumstances.

Let us deal with a few plain truths. Maybe awhile ago you owned a luxurious car but now, because you could not maintain it due to a financial crunch, you have a long walk to your office each day. Amidst all the embarrassment of the downward change in your lifestyle and standard of living, do you resign yourself to the situation and take it as God's will for you to live in such a demeaning state? If only you will have faith in the Lord, He has the power to restore that which has been taken from you.

The devil's favorite sport is to bring to ruin the God-ordained institution of marriage. Many homes are without peace. Marriage is made to last forever, but when Satan interferes, all too soon the bliss and bloom can become hazy and wavering. The devil enters the home and the peace is shattered. Everything goes downhill. The marriage boat hits the rocks, and the wind of uncertainty blows in every direction. Is that what you call God's best for you? Your zero hour might well take this form — but you should realize that God is still standing by to bring peace, harmony, and fruitfulness to every part of your life.

Despite the circumstances of your life, there is still power for your zero hour.

Opportunities for Victory

The moment you discover that there is power available to help you through your zero hour, you will see boundless opportunities to discover God's plan for fulfillment, achievement, and complete victory.

Was it God's plan that you stand all alone in your moment of difficulty? I don't think so, because He says in His Word, "I will never leave you nor forsake you." (Heb. 13:5.) Do you desire to be an achiever? Then I am convinced that no obstacle should be allowed to stop your forward victory march through Christ.

There are abundant possibilities for breakthrough in every facet of human endeavor, if the Word of God is believed and acted upon.

Many disturbing obstacles cropped up early in my ministry, but I survived the storms. "Take it easy, life is full of ups and downs," some friends tried to convince me. When I would come up against a hurdle, they would sit me down and deliver a lecture: "We have been in the ministry longer than you have. You need to mellow. You are too small for the grand plans you have set for yourself. You can never make it." But I was never tied down by their negativism.

As a young preacher, I was never content with only God's least. It will do you good to have a similar attitude. Let no force on earth, no zero hour or difficult circumstance, deter you from attaining God's best. You will climb the highest peak, go through the deepest valley, if only you believe that there is power set aside to defend you in the tough hours when all else fails you and all others desert you.

Take God's Word for It

Have you ever taken the time to search the Bible to discover what God says about you? So many Christians receive the truths of God secondhand. Try a search today! The Bible will reveal to you a God of majesty, power, and unsearchable accuracy in the management of His creation, including *your* life. The whole process of your thinking — the entire working of your mind — must be renewed and regenerated by God's quickening Word made manifest through Jesus

Christ. (Col. 1:27.) Then you will be able to align your words and actions in accordance with His revealed Word and will.

In many countries where I have preached the Word of God and counseled, one discouraging posture in particular is reflected in the thinking of the people. Millions of people seem to assume that the God of creation has abandoned His works, that He sits back indifferently as the world goes down the drain. That is not my God! He cannot be the God Who sent His Son in love to die for a sinful world. He cannot be the God of the Bible! My God, the great "I AM" (Ex. 3:14), watches over His people with loving, caring eyes.

You comb your hair every day, don't you? As you comb your hair, God takes note of every strand that drops to the ground. (Luke 12:7.) That is something which even you don't pay attention to. "How could I calculate the number of hairs that fall from my head?" you may ask. But God cares about even the non-essential things like lost hair. If this is the case, then our God must also be a Father Who delights Himself in the bigger, deeper issues of our daily lives.

It is time to get this truth straight. We all agree that certain aspects of our Christian walk upset and shake us. But does that fact remove us from the presence and love of God? Does it separate us from His strength and power and glory? The walk of faith, hand in hand with God, is the best insurance against fear of the unknown, which is the lot of nearly every person on earth.

But bear in mind that it is only when you are on the path of faith that you are aware of the enemy at work against you. This is not the hour for foolhardiness or false assumptions. God has admonished us through

28

the Apostle Paul to be on our guard, **Lest Satan should get an advantage of us: for we are not ignorant of his devices** (2 Cor. 2:11). A short commentary on this verse from *Dake's Annotated Reference Bible* offers some food for thought: "The devil will take advantage of every failure of the Christian using it to get into his life and cause his downfall."[1]

This note reminds me of a popular saying which acts as a consolation for those going through difficult conditions in austere times: "The downfall of a man is not the end of his life." That's true, isn't it?

We now turn to search God's Word for scriptures which will minister to your need and open before you new vistas of revelation knowledge so you will be able to deal decisively with every obstacle that comes your way. Open up your spirit, read the text thoughtfully, and allow the Holy Spirit to imprint its truths in your mind.

The Four Lepers

The familiar text we are going to consider is found in 2 Kings 7:3-11 and concerns four lepers. (If you have a Bible, read the entire passage prayerfully and allow the Spirit of God to bring to light its hidden truths.)

The story says that when a certain city came under siege from the Syrian army camped outside, there came a great famine. In the course of time four poor lepers were thrown out of the city gate to wither away and die. Society had rejected them; they had been declared outcasts and left to rot away on the outskirts of a frightened, captive city.

---

[1]Finis Jennings Dake (Lawrenceville, GA: Dake Bible Sales, Inc., 1963), p. 193.

"Who cares?" you may ask.

The answer is: God cares. The Bible says that there is a God Who neither sleeps nor slumbers. (Ps. 121:4.) It is He Who watches over His flock by day and night to bring to pass every plan laid out for the lives of His children. The hour of decision was near for the four lepers. But death was not God's plan for them in their zero hour. Instead He offered them life.

It is astonishing to read the faith-filled words they spoke and to note the decisive action they took:

> ...Why sit we here until we die?
>
> If we say, We will enter into the city, then the famine is in the city, and we shall die there: and if we sit still here, we die also. Now therefore come, and let us fall unto the host of the Syrians: if they save us alive, we shall live; and if they kill us, we shall but die.
>
> And they rose up in the twilight, to go unto the camp of the Syrians: and when they were come to the uttermost part of the camp of Syria, behold, there was no man there.
>
> And when these lepers came to the uttermost part of the camp, they went into one tent, and did eat and drink, and carried thence silver, and gold, and raiment....
>
> 2 Kings 7:3-5,8

In the natural, these men may have been poor lepers caught in the web of certain death from starvation and infected skin, but in faith they were giants. I repeat those triumphant words, "Why sit we here until we die?" (v. 3.) These words changed their future! The lepers did not throw in the towel! They believed that something good could happen if they moved forward. The fact is, they had hope, which is the God-factor in every situation.

Refuse to Be Moved

Throughout the Bible we see people who never gave up — and God never gave up on them either. Is it the same story today? Yes! The time of change has come because you now know that there is power beyond measure for your zero hour.

It is heartbreaking to find able-bodied, Spirit-filled believers bowing under pressure when they experience a sudden shift in fortunes. That approach is not God's plan. The Bible teaches us to say, **I can do all things through Christ which strengtheneth me** (Phil. 4:13). Jesus advised us to **...Have faith in God** (Mark 11:22). We need to be reminded that God remains the same, regardless of what conditions are before us. (Mal. 3:6; Heb. 13:8.)

Someone sang, "When the devil knocks at the door, ask Jesus to answer the call." Oh, how true that is!

Make up your mind not to budge or waver in your faith:

> **...For he that wavereth is like a wave of the sea driven with the wind and tossed.**
>
> **For let not that man think that he shall receive any thing of the Lord.**
>
> **James 1:6,7**

Reaffirm your faith in Christ and trust God by believing implicitly in what He has said about you. This can be done only if you understand what the Bible means when it says, **Let this mind be in you, which was also in Christ Jesus** (Phil. 2:5). Allow the mind of the Master to be the master of your mind.

What does the Bible mean by "the mind of Christ"? Jesus' mind was a mind bent to succeed, a mind in tune with the will of God, a mind of obedience in all circumstances. Let this mind be in you, and you will see hope and victory in the midst of your zero hour.

3

Holding on to God by Faith

...*"The righteous will live by faith."*

Romans 1:17 NIV

Many believers do not make full use of the treasure of God's love deposited within them. The Bible indicates that when one door closes against a believer, another door opens up to him by God's grace and power. Believers — all children of God — ought to hold fast to this noble truth.

"My case, Archbishop, is hopeless. I feel so helpless." This is sometimes what I hear: complete negativism. I hope this is not your viewpoint or confession. If the devil tells you that the end has come, take your case to the Lord — He has the final word.

Walking by Faith

No force, demon, or power of darkness can stop a person who has faith in God through the all-conquering Jesus Christ. Whatever your situation or circumstance, set your eyes by faith on the Lord, keep looking to Him, and continue looking until the tide turns in your favor.

The Apostle Peter did not know or follow this principle at first, as he walked on the Sea of Galilee toward Jesus. (Matt. 14:22-31.) Ficklemindedness and wavering faith were the cause of his undoing. In your faith walk you must watch out for these things too. Stay calm and trust in the power of God's might. Remember, **...the battle is not yours, but God's** (2 Chron. 20:15). We Christians are the apple of God's eye, and anything that touches us touches Him. (Zech. 2:8.)

As children of God, redeemed though the finished work of Jesus Christ on the cross of Calvary, we are saved by faith (Eph. 2:8,9) and afterwards live by faith. (Rom. 1:17; Gal. 2:20.) Many of those Christians who have failed did so because they refused to follow the Biblical standard of walking day by day with Christ, their Savior and Lord, in trusting faith. God's intention is that we continue triumphantly through every circumstance and situation of life.

But is it possible to accept Christ and receive salvation by faith, only to turn around and live through the arm of flesh? Beloved, it does not work:

> **This I say then, Walk in the Spirit....**
>
> **For we through the Spirit wait for the hope of righteousness by faith.**
>
> **Galatians 5:16,5**

It is clear from the above verses that looking for the hope of righteousness in Christ requires nothing less than walking in the Spirit through constant faith in Christ. To receive and appropriate the promise of power for your zero hour, you must understand the role of faith in the Christian walk.

The Gospel of John establishes that faith comprises one-half of a formula: the other half, which must always be included, takes the form of action. When Jesus speaks of faith, He refers to it as being revealed in action. This truth is illustrated by the lowering of the man "sick of the palsy" through the roof by his faithful friends (Mark 2:4), and the touching of the hem of Jesus' garment by the woman with the issue of blood (Matt. 9:20-22), whose cases we will examine later in this book.

Beloved, as a Christian, a sound understanding of faith will make a world of difference in your life.

Faith Produces Victory

Time after time, God has charged me to preach to believers everywhere that to be knocked down is not the end of the fight: a Christian may be knocked down but not knocked out. God will uplift him with His right hand of righteousness because He has promised that, **Though he fall, he shall not be utterly cast down: for the Lord upholdeth him with his hand** (Ps. 37:24).

In your walk with Christ, you need to see the zero hour as a moment of decision: it calls for tenacity of purpose to keep on walking even when your knees wobble and shake! Know within your spirit that, despite outward appearances, the situation is not hopeless.

Thank God, the Bible has the answer, as the Apostle John wrote in 1 John 5:4: **For whatsoever is born of God overcometh the world: and this is the victory that overcometh the world, even our *faith*.** We believers are born of God and are regenerated by His Spirit, as outlined in John 3:5,6 and Ephesians 4:23,24. Get this point established in your mind; it is the solid foundation upon which we will build.

"...*overcometh* the world...." This statement is as sure as it can be. God expects us as His blood-bought children to live an overcoming life, triumphing over every obstacle that blocks the road to victory.

"How is this possible?" you may ask.

I have experienced enough pruning and trimming to know that, clothed in the armor of God, a Christian can survive any onslaught of the enemy.

"...and this is the *victory*...." Read it to yourself once again. According to Scripture, victory for a believer is a foregone conclusion. This is why Jesus said, **...but be of good cheer; I have overcome the world** (John 16:33). We can understand why the Apostle John believed that the victory has been won for every Christian. Calvary was a place of victory, and victory in the name of Jesus enabled His disciples of old to march forward after Pentecost and "turn the world upside down" for Him. (Acts 17:6.)

As believers, you and I share in that supreme victory won at Calvary! We can go on, confident that through implicit faith in the name of Jesus Christ, victory is assured.

One Man's Hope

In his book *Man's Search for Meaning*, Dr. Victor Frankl gives a moving account of how he survived the horrors of imprisonment in the Nazi concentration camps at Auschwitz and Dachau. Although Dr. Frankl did not have a Christian faith, he held stubbornly to the hope of victory through all the torture.

"The prisoner who had lost faith in the future," he wrote, "was doomed. With his loss of belief in the future he also lost his spiritual hold; he let himself decline and became subject to mental and physical decay. Hope is a life resource, like food, water and air. In its absence, life ceases to have meaning and sometimes even ceases to be. Hope enables persons to rejoice in suffering."[1]

This is Dr. Frankl's observation on how you can survive your zero hour, the inevitable period of distress and hardship that comes to everyone at one time or another.

Sometimes I have wondered how the three Hebrew children stood firm in that hour of conflict and crisis when they knew the drastic consequences of disobedience to Nebuchadnezzar's decree. Today, the secret is in my heart and engulfs my whole being. As believers we stand on solid ground in these last days when God has spoken to us by His Son, **...whom he hath appointed heir of all things...**(Heb. 1:2).

The greatest bulwark of Christian hope in any area of endeavor, including the ministry, is the absolute certainty of final victory, the unshakable knowledge that in *all things* we are more than conquerors through Christ. (Rom. 8:37.) The full realization of this truth will turn you around full circle and open to you vistas of courage and indomitable faith through the power of the Son of God, enabling you to rise up out of the quagmire of depression and despair and soar to the heights of hope and joy where God wants you to live.

Do you know Who God is? The effectiveness of the power of God in your life depends on how well you understand Him and His sovereignty. I want to give you a glimpse of our God according to the Scriptures

---

[1](Boston: Beacon Press, 1962).

so you will be able to tap into His marvelous power and limitless resources. With the omnipotence of God in mind, along with his omnipresence and omniscience, let's think briefly about some of the practical implications of these attributes of God. But then, let's also consider how these attributes affect us in our everyday lives as children of the living God.

God Is Ready, Willing, and Able

A proper understanding of God's omnnipresence, His omniscience, and His omnipotence assures us that no situation exceeds His reach, no circumstance escapes His attention, and no experience is beyond His control. God is with us wherever we go, knows everything that happens to us, and, on our behalf, is able to remove every obstacle and solve every problem that faces us — no matter how great they may be.

My knowledge and understanding of this great truth makes a tremendous difference in my Christian living. I know a God Who knows me! God is all-seeing, all-wise, and all-powerful, and He is able and willing to deliver all those who put their trust in Him. That basic truth comforts every trusting child of God.

Remember, whatever your circumstance, condition or situation, you are never alone, never forgotten, never beyond hope or help.

Let us remind ourselves that nothing is too hard for God! (Gen. 18:14; Jer. 32:27.) The psalmist asked, **O Lord God of hosts, who is a strong Lord like unto thee?**...(Ps. 89:8). If all other Scripture escapes your mind in the turbulent hour, my dear friend, remember this: **Great is our Lord, and of great power: his understanding is infinite** (Ps. 147:5).

Whatever our location or situation, we can be confident of God's power and His presence with us. To be assured that God sees and knows and cares brings comfort and joy to our troubled hearts. Whether you are in a hospital room, lying upon a bed of affliction, broken-hearted over the loss of a loved one, or shaken and disillusioned because your dearest friend has rejected you, you can still say with Hagar, **...Thou God seest me...**(Gen. 16:13).

You may be reading these words in some remote area of the world or you may be feeling alone in a crowd. You need to know that there is power for the zero hour. God not only *sees* you, but He is on your side, in every need — no matter what it is.

I owe all my success to knowing God and what He can do. This knowledge is what drew the line between failure or success, between falling by the wayside or moving on in the power of God's might.

You must also know this truth about God for yourself. Nothing, absolutely nothing, is of greater value in life than knowing God and the power of His might. He is the pivot around which all else revolves. Yet the majority of people, even many confessing Christians, fail to know Him as they should.

When I speak of knowing God, I have much more in mind than knowing things *about* Him. Many people read *about* God and the power of Jesus Christ as Savior and Lord in newspapers, magazines, commentaries, books — and they have a shadowy image of the Lord. And yet they are not really personally acquainted with the Almighty, All-Knowing, Ever-Present God. These occasional, partial glimpses are no substitute for a person-to-person relationship with the living God. Go to the Bible and find out what He has promised; that knowledge will stand you in good stead in the zero hour.

Many incidents which have confronted me as a believer and minister have shaken me to the foundation, but they could not cause my downfall, because I knew God and His power on a personal basis. Do you?

Choose to put God first and He will give strength and direction to your life. This choice becomes a compass by which the course of life and its victory is charted. Every other decision ought to be secondary to that of choosing God. If you make the Lord your first and best, He will make you His first and best — any hour, any day. To put God first adds strength to one's character. It provides assurance of God's help in doing right. So also it adds a quality of life which cannot be destroyed. I speak from experience, because at a turning point in my life and ministry, God helped me around every tight corner.

Holding on to God

I grew up in Benin City, Nigeria, many years before independence came to that African nation. In many areas of my life, I had every encouragement one could possibly lay claim to. But life was not easy in my family although I tried to make the best of it. We were poor and the future looked bleak. I was never one to indulge in wishful thinking, but deep in my heart I knew that a change had to come some day, some how. I had convinced myself that hard work would bring a good harvest to anyone, so I put all my energies into my job of transporting goods in a wheelbarrow for a fee.

Every morning my mind would go to the success that lay ahead of me by God's grace in my daily work as a barrow-boy. It was not easy, but there has never been an easy way to success; it has always been a hard road to travel.

Someone has noted that since we expect to spend the rest of our lives in the future, we ought to be assured of what kind of future it will be. Do you want to be sure? The answer is straightforward hard work and the abiding grace of God.

Benin City, capital of Bendel State, Nigeria, has, since my youth, gone through a massive facelift, and has undergone vast social change; it found new prosperity as a result of the oil boom. Today, it is characterized by beautiful mansions and well-kept lawns, first-class roads full of modern vehicles, and people striding confidently along busy streets. The Benin City of today is not the Benin City of old; civilization has given it a new coat.

Every morning I would be on my way — with a determination to succeed where others had failed. I pushed my way through the morning crowds with my wooden barrow. If I could work hard, and do as much as my strength permitted, God would add His grace. This was my firm conviction and my charter of service. I allowed nothing to distract me as the day went on, believing that as God was with me, success would be waiting for me at the end of the way.

It has been said that true vision is an inspired look at reality. And some time ago Bob Mumford wrote in a *Life Changers* newsletter: "Vision is more than understanding, revelation or knowledge, though it may be all of these. Vision is seeing in our mind's eye the present as God sees it, as well as seeing the future of God's purpose as an accomplished fact. It is the ability not only to look at an empty field and the hidden treasure, but also to see how to acquire that field and obtain the treasure."

If ever there was a young man determined to succeed through struggle at every step, I was the one. And new vision opened up with God's help.

One day I painted the word "Opel" on the side of my cart, so that traders looking for quick service could easily identify it. Before long, I had effectively established myself as the barrow-boy who carried foodstuffs with the greatest security in the quickest possible time. Market women sought me, and traders longed to see me at dawn behind my "Opel" truck.

In all this, God was weaving a new pathway to greater heights. Many nights, as I lay in bed counting the ceiling nails to while away the time, I would feel exhaustion in my body and excruciating pain in my aching back; fatigue was taking its toll on me.

"I must do something about this condition, change my job," I pondered.

Another holiday arrived, and I made my decision: "I must have a go at being a vendor."

So I rose each morning before anyone in the compound and made my way to the Vendor's Office. I was following a demanding schedule, dividing my time between selling newspapers and rushing over to push my barrow at the market as the early traders arrived. Though I worked long, hard hours, day after day, giving up was not a part of my vocabulary. I knew everything about success, but nothing of failure. And on the day I married, I knew that God had blessed the work of my hands through the labor and toil of the past. From the black moments in the mud-thatched class-room through to the scorching sun-filled months of pushing my barrow at Oba market, everything worked together by God's grace to lay the solid foundation for a better tomorrow.

That's how God dealt with me. How did He deal with people in Bible days; what lessons are learned from *their* lives? You will find out later in this book when we begin to examine in detail the examples of several Bible characters whose faith and devotion are worthy of our study and emulation.

God's Hall of Fame and Faith

The epistles, especially the book of Hebrews, Chapter 11, offer much food for thought. Reading through Hebrews 11:17-40, we marvel at the exploits of those courageous saints of old who stood on the Lord's side. This glorious chapter is God's hall of fame and faith! Often I have read and meditated upon it; occasionally I have preached on it. Its impact, impression, and influence on my life and ministry have grown with every sermon.

Hebrews 11 makes fascinating reading as it presents a stirring account of the toils, trials, and tribulations of the Biblical saints:

> **Who through faith subdued kingdoms, wrought righteousness, obtained promises, stopped the mouths of lions,**
>
> **Quenched the violence of fire, escaped the edge of the sword, out of weakness were made strong, waxed valiant in fight, turned to flight the armies of the aliens,**
>
> **...received their dead raised to life again:...were tortured....**

...were stoned,...sawn asunder,...being destitute, afflicted, tormented;

And these all, having obtained a good report through faith, received not the promise.

Hebrews 11:33-35,37,39

Perhaps you are wondering what lay behind these fabulous testimonies? Power to withstand comes only through knowledge of God, which in turn gives rise to faith in Him. Daniel 11:32 declares boldly: **...but the people that *do know* their God shall be strong, and do exploits.**

Trust in the Lord

This is the age of cynicism, discouragement, doubt, scepticism, uncertainty, and unreality, but you will not get far in your walk with God if you allow these negative forces to control you and become part of your speech. Cynicism is born out of disillusionment which hoped for an immediate answer, but found nothing. Things may not always turn out as we expect, but that does not alter the fact that as God's dear children, He is in control of our lives.

Trust in the Lord. Look not at circumstances. Do not judge God by your feelings, but by faith, for **...without faith it is impossible to please him: for he that cometh to God must believe that he is, and that he is a rewarder of them that diligently seek him** (Heb. 11:6).

The bizarre and hazy ideas that occasionally float into our heads are all efforts by the enemy to sow seeds of doubt in our minds which he hopes will germinate and grow into unbelief. Do you sometimes feel uncertain? You may, but that experience changes neither the fact of God's sovereignty nor the strength of the power which He puts at our disposal. Uncertainty is the inability to find something secure on which to place one's faith. A believing Christian has something secure upon which to anchor his faith: *God*. **The name of the Lord is a strong tower: the righteous runneth into it, and is safe** (Prov. 18:10).

An inability to discern God's goals and intentions through the circumstances which He permits to come into our life acts as a hindrance to spiritual growth. Picture a new Christian who has just accepted the Lord. Rapidly and unexpectedly, everything in his life starts to go haywire — the bills begin to pile up, he has trouble with his wife and children, and a good neighbor suddenly becomes aggressive. The new believer begins to wonder if he has made the right decision in accepting Christ. But no one can convince me that these developments are outside of the knowledge, concern, or power of God. The new Christian should simply settle down and take it easy, secure in the fact that as he follows the Lord in full faith and confidence, all these things will sort themselves out in good time.

Often God uses circumstances to help us find Him or His will for us. If we are unable to discern what God is trying to do in our lives, we will spend years being miserable and defeated. Every problem you face has a purpose. It moves you one step ahead. It builds you up so **...that ye may be able to bear it.**

> **There hath no temptation taken you but such as is common to man: but God is faithful, who will not suffer you to be tempted above that ye are able; but will with the temptation also make a way to escape, that ye may be able to bear it.**
>
> **1 Corinthians 10:13**

Beloved, there is power for your zero hour which enables you to master your problems, bring back life, restore the wasted years, and nourish new hope. This power gives you the privilege of knowing that God is taking you into His confidence.

4

Abraham: The Father of Faith

**Now faith is being sure of what we hope for and
certain of what we do not see. This is what the ancients
were commended for.**

Hebrews 11:1 NIV

Several years ago the Lord gave me a new insight
into the subject of faith. The Holy Spirit led me to the
thirteenth chapter of Genesis, where we find an
account of the patriarch Abraham.

Every story about Abraham reveals a consistent
faith-walk with God. It is therefore no exaggeration
when he is called the "father of our faith." (Rom. 4:1.)
Abraham also had the singular privilege and honor of
being called the "friend of God." (James 2:23.) Abraham
was mightily blessed of God and was exceedingly
wealthy. God honors and blesses all His people, but
Abraham was prospered of the Lord in a dimension
and magnitude which is almost beyond our modern-
day comprehension. He had no equal in all the world!

The Faith of Abraham

The finest thing about Abraham was his faith. But
let us not think of faith as magic, as a charm by which
to obtain something we want. Faith is not a magic wand
with which to bring God under a spell and get from
Him that which satisfies us. Instead, as Abraham
discovered, faith means approaching God with firm

confidence, humility, and submission, asking for the blessing that is needed in order to fulfill the purpose He has for us, or to carry out the mission He has assigned to us.

This kind of faith is the key to abundant blessing, greater blessings than we even imagine. God blessed Abraham beyond measure: his household, servants, cattle, and everything he owned were cared for by God's loving hands.

In Genesis 13:2 we read: **And Abram was very rich in cattle, in silver, and in gold.** The people of his day looked to Abraham as a symbol of God's provision; and, sure enough, he lived in abundant prosperity every moment of his life. But many Christians miss one prominent point about Father Abraham: his obedience and faith. Abraham was aware of God at all times and remained constantly in submission to Him and His divine will.

Abraham was a great man of faith and obedience. These two grand principles controlled his life.

God called Abraham in much the same way as you and I receive the call to do one thing or another for Him today. When we consider what Abraham was being called *from* (a good land, friends, kith and kin, an established dwelling) and what he was being called *to* (arduous journeyings, an unknown land, the nomadic life of a pioneer), we can appreciate the rigors of the test that God was placing before him.

But the Almighty also gave Abraham great and precious promises. So Abraham was willing to break the ties of his former life and move on in faith to a new experience. The mountaintop of faith on which

Abraham dwelt was at far too high an elevation for such a man as his nephew Lot — and would be too high for many Christians today.

Abraham might have looked up into the starry sky and sighed, "What a mighty God we serve; heaven and earth adore Him." Abraham had everything a man could wish for and more. By faith in God, he saw only glory, glory, glory. Then, with the swiftness of an arrow through a dark night, the crisis came. Abraham ran into rough waters, and uncertainty marred his glorious view. The riches and blessings suddenly became a burden:

> **And there was a strife between the herdmen of Abram's cattle and the herdmen of Lot's cattle....**
>
> **And Abram said unto Lot, Let there be no strife....**
>
> **Is not the whole land before thee? separate thyself, I pray thee, from me: if thou wilt take the left hand, then I will go to the right; or if thou depart to the right hand, then I will go to the left.**
>
> **Genesis 13:7-9**

Every word speaks of absolute submission on the part of Abraham. There was no trace whatsoever of panic or anxiety. Oh, how I pray that all believers will take his cool-headedness as their example. Many Christians run around in fear and panic when a crisis comes; they make wrong decisions and ruin their lives. Father Abraham gave Lot the opportunity to take the choicest portion of the land. He had no fear. Immediately after Abraham had made this agreement with Lot, we read these words: **And the Lord said unto Abram...**(Gen. 13:14). The reason Abraham was so confident and so free of fear and anxiety was because he knew that God was right there beside him to guide, protect, and bless him whichever way he went.

There are certain hidden truths in the nature and character of the two men, Abraham and Lot, which we must take note of. These truths are as relevant in our day as they were in the days of the Old Testament.

Abraham, in his wisdom, represents the truly faithful, obedient follower of the Lord. He was growing in grace and following the Lord every step of the way. As with Abraham, God still wants to reveal Himself to His people through everyday circumstances and happenings. It is His purpose to do so, and we must be aware of it.

Lot represents, no doubt, those who believe and are justified (2 Pet. 2:7,8), and are therefore saved from death, but who nevertheless want to hold on to the things of this world — its pleasures and attractions. These, the worldly-minded, God has to continually push forward to keep them moving in the right direction, as the angel did with Lot in Sodom and Gomorrah.

Lot chose for himself: God chose for Abraham. Which of the two received the most in the long run? Abraham, by far. In this crisis-infested generation in which we live, it pays to let God do our choosing and provide our solutions.

To Be on the Lord's Side

God knows those who trust in Him. Are you one of them? The answer to God's divine choice and call is remarkably evident in Abraham's case:

> **And the Lord said unto Abram, after that Lot was separated from him, Lift up now thine eyes....**
>
> **For all the land which thou seest, to thee will I give it....**

> **And I will make thy seed as the dust of the earth....**
>
> **Arise, walk through the land...; for I will give it unto thee.**
>
> **Genesis 13:14-17**

Now I pose the inevitable question: to whom do you turn whenever a problem arises in your life like a storm on a calm sea? When the peace is broken, the truce is shattered, and an unwanted confrontation stares you in the face, whom do you call upon in that zero hour? The psalmist wrote of those among whom he dwelled: **I am for peace: but when I speak, they are for war** (Ps. 120:7). The world has not changed, man has not changed, but those who change the world are the ones who hear from God.

Abraham found his shelter in the Lord. David had the same answer. After all the trials he had endured in life, the "sweet singer of Israel" wrote of the Lord: **He shall cover thee with his feathers, and under his wings shalt thou trust...**(Ps. 91:4).

This psalm, notably verse 4, reminds me of a scene I once came upon during a rainstorm. The raindrops were hitting me with the force of arrows, and since home was far away, I decided to seek shelter behind an old school building.

As I wiped off the drops of rain, I saw just a little distance away a hen perched over her chicks to protect them from the rain and cold. By fluttering her wings, the hen warned me to keep away, which I did. During the long period I stood there, the hen preached a whole sermon to me. Even a hen takes needless trouble to protect her chicks and keep them safe. Yet we serve an Almighty God Who has the whole universe in His hands. Therefore, like the psalmist of old, we should say, "I shall not fear." This is what Psalm 91:4 is assuring us today: "He shall cover thee with his feathers, and under his wings shalt thou trust...." What a comforting picture of God, covering us with His feathers and the wings of His forgiving love and providential care as exhibited in Christ:

> **Nay, in all these things we are more than conquerors through him that loved us.**
>
> **For I am persuaded, that neither death, nor life, nor angels, nor principalities, nor powers, nor things present, nor things to come,**
>
> **Nor height, nor depth, nor any other creature, shall be able to separate us from the love of God, which is in Christ Jesus our Lord.**
>
> **Romans 8:37-39**

Someone has counted 365 "fear nots" in the Bible. This good news is for all fear-filled days. There is a new message of hope for each day of our life. Abraham came face to face with his zero hour, a moment of decision with far-reaching consequences. God sanctioned Abraham's separation from Lot, and then came a miracle of blessing. If we will only obey God and walk in His ways and precepts, no good thing will He withhold from us. (Ps. 84:11.)

Blessing Follows Obedience

Abraham discovered that blessing follows faithful obedience to God, and so he departed and never looked back. As a result, God said to him, **I will make thy seed as the dust of the earth....walk through the land...for I will give it unto thee.** We can now fully understand why the Bible says that every good and perfect gift comes from God. (James 1:17.) The Lord proved it in the life of Abraham.

My friend, are you going to trust God in the crisis facing you? Or do you think you can cope alone? It does not work out that way.

What did Abraham have which we so badly need today? He had a teachable mind, a surrendered will, and a committed life: all these are basic conditions for a fruitful walk with God at all times.

Today we may surrender ourselves to a task, but tomorrow, when something goes wrong, either we blame God or we give up. Time and time again, I have met individuals who surrendered to the task of preaching the Gospel, carrying out a ministerial responsibility, undertaking a Christian duty. Later, when difficulties arose or the inevitable zero hour came, they gave up and "went back to Egypt." When hurdles arose they ended their Christian ministry. What they should do in the first place is to surrender to *God*, rather than to the task.

Failure to see this truth leads to discouragement. Difficulties will come regardless of what type of work we are in, but if our surrender is to the Lord instead of to the task, we will look at obstacles from quite a different perspective.

You may be laboring, groaning, and crying out to the Lord, "My business losses, my marriage troubles, my family woes, my financial crises, my health problems!" The "my" in your petition removes God from you. "My" in the absence of God becomes "my" on the way to destruction.

Turning to God

When trouble came, Abraham did the right thing; he quickly turned to God Who picked up the broken pieces of his life. God assured Abraham, "Friend, let us start all over again." Abraham bowed to God's grand proposition and humbly followed His direction.

All over the world, in every culture and society and among every class of people, the experience of being born again creates a wall of demarcation, even a wall of separation, between the believer and the world. And this division underscores the Bible commandment, **Wherefore come out from among them, and be ye separate, saith the Lord...**(2 Cor. 6:17).

If you know anything about the Corinthian church, you will understand why God gave the order through Paul to come out and be separate. This is not separation as many unregenerate minds consider it; we are not all commanded to become monks or hermits, to exclude ourselves from society in a monastery or on an isolated hilltop. This is not what the Bible means by separation. What the Scriptures mean when they speak of separation from the world is the fact that our renewed and regenerated mind does not conform any more to this world's standards. We don't think as the world thinks, neither do we behave as it behaves. Our aspirations are geared to fulfilling God's purposes, not our own selfish ambitions. This change comes from walking every day in fresh realization of God's will and plans for our life.

We have all heard of believers who have been rejected by their families. Sometimes your relatives will no longer speak to you when you choose to follow the path of righteousness and the way of the Lord. But have no regret, for if you stand steadfast, and prove faithful to the calling of God, your brethren will come knocking at your door seeking counsel. It happened to Joseph, and it can happen to you.

David Livingstone, the great missionary, had a moving story to tell and a living testimony relevant to every believer. After graduating from the university, he felt the call of God to Africa. With that call came an earnest, burning desire to serve the Lord and bring the light of Jesus Christ to the Dark Continent.

"I am preparing to sail to Africa and take the Good News to the blacks," Livingstone told a university colleague as they walked together one evening.

Suddenly, as if bitten by a rattlesnake, and with the finesse of an Olympic gold medalist, his friend sprang away and landed on the other side of the sidewalk. He stood staring at Livingstone with a reddened face and a shocked expression.

"Livingstone, what is the matter with you?" the colleague asked incredulously. "Are you *normal?*"

Livingstone walked over to his friend and, with the characteristic calmness of a thoroughbred Christian set on a divine commission, just nodded his head in affirmation, stating, "I must go to Africa!"

Shaking his head in disbelief, the colleague, with renewed fervor and confidence, retorted, "Well, *I* am going to stay in London, go into business, and make a name for myself."

Livingstone died in the jungles of Africa sharing the love of God with poor underprivileged people, but his death brought the whole of England to a standstill. A special ship brought home his remains. He was honored posthumously and millions filed past his coffin to pay homage to a man who stood for God. His body was ceremoniously carried to Westminster Abbey, the last resting place of many great men of renown.

Today, David Livingstone has a place in history; he has left an indelible mark. His boastful and conceited friend died forgotten and unsung.

If you will only stand for God when the moment of decision comes, the great "I AM" will not forsake you.

Your Moment of Decision

There may be times when your colleagues will desert you, and your family and loved ones no longer trust you, because the cross is an offense to them. Even your oldest and dearest friends may no longer confide in you. Suddenly, you become a scarecrow, an object of ridicule and scorn.

"How can anyone be so foolish as to depend upon God alone?" they may ponder as you pass by on your way to church. They may even feel that you have a few screws loose in your head. "This cannot be just ordinary religion, it must be a fanatical sect," they may conclude as they stand in judgment upon you.

But listen, my friend! If your conversion is real and thorough, your family and friends will eventually resolve to find out more about it. They will keep searching day after day to discover what you have that they don't. Be faithful and obedient, steadfast in all things. Yours is a God Who can be depended upon. Lean totally upon Him. Trust and hold to Him in every situation and circumstance of life and you will emerge victorious.

As a faithful Christian, you are discovering God's power for every need. This truth is testified to by His Word: **Many are the afflictions of the righteous: but the Lord delivereth him out of them all** (Ps. 34:19).

Beloved, you will not fall as your enemies expect, because the eye of the Lord is upon you. People may spend eternity searching for your secret, and yet, if you are solidly anchored in God, they will never find it. Why? Because you *have* no special secret of your own, simply the principle: **...The just shall live by faith** (Rom. 1:17).

But this fact is not easy for the unsaved to understand, let alone believe, because the carnal mind cannot fathom spiritual things. (Rom. 8:7; 1 Cor. 2:14.) Let not your heart be troubled as the world mocks, jeers, and spites you. Jesus Christ set the standard, and as His follower you cannot be excluded from suffering. Why do you allow the sneers to bother you?

"Church in the morning, church in the evening, church, church, church. Why?" That is the kind of taunt you may hear from those who misunderstand and oppose you. But let your faith stand on God alone. He knows your situation and your labor. He sees, He cares, and He will reward you in the end. (Heb. 6:10.)

The zero hour sometimes arrives unexpectedly and throws many Christians off balance. How will you react in the time of crisis? With the hasty insistence of Lot's decision to break away from peaceful Abraham? (Gen. 13.) Will you feel shock and dread as did Hezekiah? (Is. 38.) Your zero hour could be far more lethal and exacting, as the abruptness of Saul's deadly javelin launched at innocent David. (1 Sam. 18:11.) Think of repentant Rahab, who had hidden the spies of Israel, as she waited for the invasion of the Israelites in that little house by the Jericho wall.

"My goodness, the walls are crumbling," she might easily have sighed tearfully as the battle began. "My whole world is coming to an end!" That was her zero hour. But she came through it unscathed because she had been honest and faithful to the Lord and His servants.

The breakthrough in all these seemingly hopeless and separate moments is brought about by a reaction which might be called the "faith move." Read the chapters in the Bible involving Abraham, Hezekiah, David, and Rahab, and you will be astonished to discover how much they trusted God.

In Philippians 4:6 (NIV) the Apostle Paul says, Do not be anxious about anything.... These men and women knew how to trust God Whose power was enough for any upheaval. Fear and anxiety may force you to make a false move, but remember, "Where there is faith, there is no fear."

Be as Faithful as Abraham

God called Abraham and said, **Arise, walk through the land in the length of it and in the breadth of it; for I will give it into thee** (Gen. 13:17).

Immediately after the incident between Abraham and Lot, God told Abraham to arise. He obeyed. Instead, Abraham might have sat down wondering, "Oh, what's the use after this misfortune that has befallen me?" But no, God told His servant to stand up and put on a cheerful countenance, because tragedy was to open the door to great blessings.

Have you ever noticed that God did not give the expanse of land to Abraham until *after* he had braved his zero hour? It will be the same for you. Right now, before your very eyes, the crisis — that storm thundering around you — will become a door to God's fruitful abundance and a new pathway to untold blessings.

In Deuteronomy 6:4,5, all of Israel was called to attention. Today the same passage speaks to all believers in Christ:

> **Hear, O Israel, the Lord our God is one Lord:**
>
> **And thou shalt love the Lord thy God with all thine heart, and with all thy soul, and with all thy might.**

This is the greatest commandment of all. (Matt. 22:34-40.) Abraham was obedient to it all his life, and God honored him. We should follow Abraham's example: God should be first in our thinking, first in our affections, first in our loyalty, first in our service, first in everything! As King David wrote in Psalm 20:7,8:

> **Some trust in chariots, and some in horses: but we will remember the name of the Lord our God.**
>
> **They are brought down and fallen: but we are risen, and stand upright.**

There are thousands who have graduated from a zero hour to prosperous times. Abraham is one of them. He received power from God because the Lord had made a covenant with him. The Bible says that, from a point of distress and near deprivation, Abraham rose to a position of prominence and plenty. What was his secret? He turned from the world to the Almighty God Who can do all things by His might and power.

"Winners never quit, and quitters never win." So goes the saying. This thought gives us a clue to Abraham's success. The Bible says, **...Go, and do thou likewise** (Luke 10:37). A study of the life of Abraham will impress upon you the basic lessons you need to know in order to come through your zero hour into the life of joy and abundance God desires and plans for you.

5

Moses: Delivered by Faith

Some trust in chariots and some in horses, but we trust in the name of the Lord our God.

Psalm 20:7 NIV

Moses was another great man of God. His life was full of trials and temptations, but in every situation God proved Himself faithful.

The Lord raised up Moses in a most unusual manner, far beyond human comprehension. His mother was pregnant with him when a decree was issued to the effect that all male Hebrew children born in Egypt must be **...cast into the river...**(Exod. 1:22). But the Bible says that Moses' mother saw him as a "fine child" (Exod. 2:2 NIV) — in other words, a special child, to be saved by God.

I believe with all my heart that as you read this account, God will open your eyes and make *you* to see yourself as a "fine child," a "special child," a child of God carefully chosen in Jesus' name.

In my formative and adolescent years, I went through a period of deprivation and rejection. On one occasion I was thrown out and left to die. But, praise God, He preserved my life. God will do the same for you, even today!

Moses was also born into a harrowing situation, under conditions of slavery and the threat of imminent death. His parents hid him for three months, and then came the hour of decision. According to the book of Acts, he too was "cast forth" (Acts 7:2). But God was aware of what was going on. He was right there with Moses and his family during every tense moment.

We thank God for faithful women like Moses' mother who listen to the Lord and act in faith. She, according to the Bible (Exod. 2:2,3), took a little ark, or basket, and with meticulous care made it waterproof by coating it with pitch inside and out. She had to act quickly because there were sentries all over the city. Then she placed her precious baby in the basket and hid it among the bulrushes at the edge of the river. I believe that Moses' mother knew that a greater power would preserve him. It was by faith that she commended him to the care of the Almighty by "casting" him into the river in that floating basket.

Listen, beloved friend, in your down-and-out moment, even your zero hour, God does not leave you alone. He doesn't desert you. God had an agent prepared to intervene in Moses' situation. This agent of God, the daughter of Pharaoh, picked up the Hebrew baby and took him with her to the palace of the king to raise him as her very own child. Everything was working out beautifully.

One fact I discovered early in my ministry is that when we become involved in a crisis, God moves every hand and agent in our direction to save us. He intervenes in our zero hour.

When the Thieves Come, God Is There

Let me digress and share with you an amazing incident which occurred some years ago.

It had been a day full of enjoyable activities and good times. My family and I had gone to bed late after entertaining a group of Christian friends. As I lay in bed, all was silent: you could have heard a pin drop. The minutes passed by and I dozed off for a few hours. Then, in what I imagined to be a dream, I heard the faint sound of hushed voices followed by the distinct noise of keys fumbling in a lock.

Sitting up on the edge of my bed, calm and collected in the darkness, I was able to confirm my suspicions: our house was being burglarized by armed robbers. As I tiptoed to the window overlooking the garden, my heart raced and sweat gathered in my palms.

I had already prayed and was confident of God's protection and security. I remembered the words of the prophet, **No weapon that is formed against thee shall prosper...**(Is. 54:17). I also recollected Psalm 20:7 about trusting in the Lord, and Revelation 12:11 which states that the saints overcame the enemy **...by the blood of the Lamb, and by the word of their testimony....** Then I recited to myself the words of Deuteronomy 28:7: **The Lord shall cause thine enemies that rise up against thee to be smitten before thy face....**

I looked around to see my wife sleeping soundly, oblivious to all the drama unfurling around her. I decided to make a check of our main hall. Gathering all my courage, I crept into the dark hallway and switched on the light. There I stood, face to face, with four trigger-happy armed robbers. I greeted them; there was no reply, instead they pointed their guns at me. The leader of the gang barked out threateningly, "Bring all your money or we'll kill you now!"

I evaded their instructions by boldly firing back with the words: "Do you know whose house you have come to rob?"

The leader looked at me with angry, bloodshot eyes and answered impetuously, "This is the house of Archbishop Idahosa."

I knew it was time to act quickly. Their unblinking eyes were fixed on me. Their fingers were ready on their triggers. Tension filled the air. But I knew that God was in control because my life is in His hands. I moved a few uneven strides forward and they moved a step or two backwards towards the wall. They were on the defensive, but God was winning — I knew it!

Suddenly I shouted, "You want to rob Archbishop Idahosa — wait for me to get my weapon!"

I uttered these words with unexpected faith and force, and then dashed off at top speed into the bedroom. I laid hold of my big Bible and ran back to face the four men. I lifted up the Bible in the direction of the leader, and without further ceremony or word they fled from the house, bumping into each other as they went. Soon afterwards, the sound of a car engine broke the nighttime silence. They had gone.

This dramatic midnight incident may raise a laugh today, but it put me in a very tight spot at the time; indeed it was a zero hour. To my great joy, God stood by me in that dark hour. And He will do the same for you in your "dark hours."

God Is Where God Is

Let's return to Moses. His mother, by faith, took a firm hold on God's sovereignty. Moses was not old enough to have said, "God help me in this hour." But his mother entrusted him to God's providential care. His parents did what God wanted them to do, and He honored their faith.

If you walk in the center of God's will, He will keep you going, regardless of the storms that may assail you. The very hour that Moses was placed in the water, God's mighty machinery of protection was set in motion.

A great drama was unfolding. We learn in the second chapter of Exodus that Pharaoh's daughter came down to bathe in the river, caught sight of the basket, and commanded her servants to bring it to her. Immediately her heart was touched, and she was overcome with compassion. With loving, tender hands the princess picked up the little boy. She no doubt recognized the infant as a Hebrew child, but had no hesitation in taking him in, even at the risk of her own position. God was moving systematically, as He always does, to protect His children who trust Him in time of danger, persecution, and affliction.

Pharaoh's daughter gladly accepted the suggestion of Miriam, Moses' older sister who was watching over him, that she go and find a Hebrew woman to look after the child.

Can you imagine that? The Bible says, **...with God nothing shall be impossible** (Luke 1:37). This story fills my heart with awe, bringing to my mind the words of the old hymn, "God works in mysterious ways, His wonders to perform."

Miriam went and called Moses' mother to come and take care of her own son!

> And Pharaoh's daughter said unto her, Take this child away, and nurse it for me, and I will give thee thy wages. And the woman took the child, and nursed it.
>
> And the child grew, and she brought him unto Pharaoh's daughter, and he became her son. And she called his name Moses: and she said, Because I drew him out of the water.
>
> Exodus 2:9,10

And so, Moses moved from slavery to royalty. I believe that God cast a veil over the eyes of Pharaoh's daughter so she did not recognize that the child belonged to his mother. Instead, she took him into the palace and agreed to foot every bill for his education and training. This is what God can do for you in your life, in the bleak and shadowy moments when all else fails. God is alive and well and on your side.

Beloved friend, every word in the Bible is true! It was written **...by inspiration of God...**(2 Tim. 3:16). If you will only believe, and act upon it by faith, I can assure you in the name of the Lord that this decision will mark the turning point in your life. Forward march to victory, triumphing over every hurdle and obstacle!

> Be strong and of a good courage, fear not, nor be afraid of them: for the Lord thy God, he it is that doth go with thee; he will not fail thee, nor forsake thee.
>
> Deuteronomy 31:6

When you don't know what to do or where to turn, be confident of this one truth, and don't sell it at any price: there is a God Who cares and Whose eyes search around the earth — east, west, north, and south — seeking whom He can bless. (2 Chron. 16:9.) Remember this also: even when no brother or sister is there with you in your situation, God is always there and cares more than you can ever imagine.

God's Divine Presence

The power of God is effective beyond measure when we choose to use it by faith. This is precisely what Moses' mother did, and God stood by her. The Lord covered the eyes of the palace officials for forty years! Moses and his parents lived right under the nose of Pharaoh. And yet they were the very people the king wanted to kill.

Pharaoh took Moses as his own firstborn son and made him leader of Egypt. Moses commanded the army of Pharaoh. In the midst of enemy territory, God gave Moses victory — when he should have been beaten down and forgotten. Moses received a personal assignment from the Lord; he was to lead the Israelites out of Egypt. He was called to a frighteningly difficult but exceedingly glorious task. No wonder he felt inadequate. His lame excuses displeased the Lord, but Moses was willing to learn, whatever the cost.

God promised Moses His unfailing presence: **...Certainly I will be with thee...**(Exod. 3:12). That's what we want to hear today. But many are crying and complaining so much that they don't hear God's promise of His divine presence, which is a sure guarantee of success. When we accept a divine call, we must also claim divine help.

We see Moses struggling to evade the Master's call. He wanted to know God's name because he was sure that the children of Israel were bound to ask who had sent him. The paganism, idolatry, and heathenism of Egypt had corrupted the religion of the Hebrews. God gave His name as "I AM." (Exod. 3:14.) He is a fact, a reality. He is a person — eternal, unchangeable, self-contained, and self-sufficient. He cannot be explained or defined by anything outside Himself. Quite obviously, the name "I AM" was meant to convey a new and precious revelation. It is as full of meaning for you and me as it was for Moses.

Faith in the Great "I AM"

The majestic name "I AM" enables us to glimpse the unmerited grace of God. "I AM" is an unfinished sentence. It has no object. "I AM" — what? It is marvelous to discover from the Bible that God is saying, "I AM...whatever My people need!" The sentence is left unfinished so that man can bring his many needs, as they arise, to complete it!

One Christian writer has stated that without human need this great name of God goes around and around in a closed circle. According to him, the name "I AM that I AM" (Exod. 3:14) makes God incomprehensible. But, he points out, as soon as human needs are presented, then the Lord becomes whatever is lacking. At that point the sentence has an object, the thought is completed, and the true nature of God is revealed.

Do you lack peace? "I am thy peace **Jehovah-shalom,**" says the Lord. (Judges 6:24.) Do you lack strength? "I am thy strength" **(the strength of Israel)** says God. (1 Sam. 15:29.) Do you lack spiritual life? "I am thy life." (John 14:6.) Do you lack wisdom. "I am thy wisdom." (1 Cor. 1:30.) Do you lack righteousness? "I am thy righteousness." (Jer. 23:6.)

The name "I AM" is like a blank check. Our faith can fill in whatever the Lord is to us personally. Whatever we lack, He is. Just as water always seeks the lowest level, so the great "I AM" always seeks to fill our greatest need. He is forever "I AM...that which My people need."

God will lift you up to where the eagles soar as you begin to understand your authority in Him over every shortcoming, and as you grasp His power to redeem and restore you. As the Apostle Paul told the Ephesians, I also pray: **That the God of our Lord Jesus Christ, the Father of glory, may give unto you the spirit of wisdom and revelation in the knowledge of him** (Eph. 1:17).

Although trials, temptations, and problems are the lot of man, some are clearly avoidable. Many of them block mankind's forward march to success and victory, causing many people to fall by the wayside, give up, or just hobble through life. But this ought not to be so. It is not God's plan and will for us as human beings.

In the great "I AM" there is ample provision for every need of life.

God's Love Never Fails

God loves us, and cares about us, regardless of the crisis in which we may find ourselves. This is the believer's hope — faith in God. (Heb. 11:1.)

Beloved, if you trust in God as your loving heavenly Father, you can have positive faith that He will not allow your problems to crush you. God has a great investment in you. He has a definite plan for you, and learning through your problems is part of that plan.

The Bible calls believers *joint-heirs with Christ,* and promises that if we suffer with Him, we will also be glorified with Him. (Rom. 8:17.) Think of your zero hours as the pages of a new textbook. They may not be fun to leaf through, but they are full of valuable information. Have confidence that by the time you have reached the last page, it will be time for you to graduate!

The Apostle Paul kept his mind on Christ, **the author and finisher of our faith.** (Heb. 12:2.) Even his days in prison were transformed into a time of beautiful and refreshing inspiration. Self-pity will do you no good. Bear in mind the testimony of Paul:

> ...this one thing I do, forgetting those things which are behind, and reaching forth unto those things which are before,
>
> I press toward the mark for the prize of the high calling of God in Christ Jesus.
>
> Philippians 3:13,14

Throughout my ministry, I too have been rocked, time and time again, by crises — some of them inevitable. But now I know that when trials come, double victory follows.

Faith in the Hour of Crisis

Some years ago, the eight churches of Benin City which we had founded went through a time of great tribulation. God woke me one night and said, "Now that you are receiving national publicity, now that you are known in the nineteen states of Nigeria, take advantage of this publicity and hold more crusades and open more churches."

"But Lord," I protested, "what of the reproach that has come upon me?"

"You go not in your name," He answered, "you go in My name. You don't preach yourself, you preach Me. And if you preach Me, people will come to find out whether you are still standing or not. They will come to see whether the tribulations and the trials have brought you down, or whether you have survived them."

So in obedience to the Lord's command, I called the pastors in Benin City and told them what God had said.

"Just open more churches," I said. "Open more branches."

But then I prayed, "Lord, the people will not come because I am being criticized everywhere. Oh, God, how am I going to face it? Can I ever stand again and preach?"

The Lord responded, "When My Son was accused and abused, I gave Him a name above all names. At the name of Jesus every knee will bow and every tongue confess that Jesus Christ is Lord." (Phil. 2:10,11.)

So we opened another branch, which was church number nine. Then came the tenth. In 1982 we opened the eleventh church in Benin City. By 1986 we had fifty-one branches of the Church of God Mission in that city. And the work is still growing and progressing. Why? Because God has continued to open new doors for us.

I see God planning victory for you today. He wants to do something good in your life, too. God wants to put a smile on your face so that you can testify with the Apostle Paul: **Now thanks be unto God, which**

71

always causeth us to triumph in Christ, and maketh manifest the savour of his knowledge by us in every place (2 Cor. 2:14).

The zero hours are bound to come your way, no matter how spiritual you are, no matter how faithfully you practice the principles of Scripture in your life. But lift your eyes and stand up; you are not alone. If God be with you, who can be against you? (Rom. 8:31).

6

The Woman With the Issue of Blood: Faith Brings Wholeness

..."Daughter, your faith has healed you. Go in peace."

Luke 8:48 NIV

The woman who touched the hem of Jesus' garment in faith was made whole. (Mark 5:25-34; Luke 8:43-48.)

This Bible story will show you how to release your faith even in the most difficult conditions. Once you have done so, your faith will in turn release healing power, causing it to flow into your being to destroy disease and affliction.

The Bible does not record the name of the woman. I think the reason is because God would have us draw courage and inspiration from her story by putting our name where hers could have been. Then we too will release our faith, not by touching the clothes of Jesus, as she did, but by using some other point of contact that will enable us to believe Christ for our deliverance and receive from Him a miracle as glorious as hers.

Seven things happened in this woman's life that can be just as real for us today:

1. *She came to the end of her own resources.*

The Bible says that this woman had suffered from an issue of blood for twelve years. (Luke 8:43.) She had an incurable disease. Perhaps it was cancer, we don't know. The Gospel of Mark tells us that she **...had suffered many things of many physicians, and had spent all that she had, and was nothing bettered, but rather grew worse** (Mark 5:26).

One day this poor, sick woman faced up to her problem and realized that she had exhausted medical science, as well as her monetary resources. She made a remarkable decision — to stop before she went to pieces. She knew where she stood; she was beyond human help. She came to the end of her own way and halted. Fear sets in when we know there is no cure for our ailment, yet we frantically keep seeking human aid. This woman wisely stopped before her fear tore her to pieces.

2. She heard the story of faith — and believed it.

The story of Jesus reached this woman's ears; she heard that there was a Galilean Prophet Who was traveling throughout Judea, healing the sick and bringing peace to their souls. So remarkable was His power that totally blind eyes had been opened by His touch; the deaf and mute now heard and spoke; even some of the hopeless cripples had been made whole.

Naturally, great crowds thronged around Him, so that He hardly had time to rest or eat. The crowds were so thick that only a few had the opportunity to talk with Him or have Him place His hands upon them. But His ministry had inspired such faith that now the people wanted only to touch Him, and it was reported that everyone who came close enough to do so was made perfectly whole.

His name? Jesus of Nazareth.

This was astounding news, but the woman believed it — every word of it. Anyone who can believe in human skill can believe in divine power. For what man can do partially, God can do completely; and what man cannot do at all, our heavenly Father can do perfectly.

The story this woman heard about Jesus of Nazareth is the same today. I believed it, and through it I found the way to faith and hope and was healed. I ask you also to believe this story of faith, for I know that through it God can do something about your frustrations, fears, and illnesses.

This woman said to herself, "How wonderful this Man must be! He heals those who just touch Him. That is the most amazing thing I have ever heard! If He can do that for them, He can do it for me."

With these words, she made her decision: if she could but touch the hem of His garment, her faith would be released, and she would be made whole.

3. *She created a faith-image of Jesus — and of being healed by Him.*

When this woman heard of Jesus and believed to the extent that she could decide upon a point of contact with Him, then He became real to her. He was no longer a mere name or a symbol of hope to others. He became a Person to her — One Who could give back her life and restore her health. Her mind was filled with Him. Long before she saw Him, all other persons had faded from her thoughts. The failures of the past were forgotten. All other hopes and schemes were discarded, all other plans laid aside. Her one goal was to make contact with Jesus.

The Bible says that when she heard of Him, **…she said, If I may touch but his clothes, I shall be whole** (Mark 5:28). She saw Him in her mind before she saw Him with her eyes. She saw herself there in His presence, touching His clothes, feeling His healing virtue, and being restored to health — all before she ever went to Him. This made her Christ-conscious. It put her in the right frame of mind to receive her healing. There was no fear in her mind because it was filled with thoughts of Jesus. She knew that the Source of her healing was a *Person,* and that when she reached out to Him in faith, she would be made whole.

4. *She touched Him for a specific reason.*

After she had touched Him and had felt that she was healed of her illness, she told Him why she had done so. Her aim was to be made whole. For that purpose she had touched Him. (Mark 5:33.)

Human life is a whole — a unit. You are made in the image of God. You have a mind with a free will. You live in a box, or house, of muscle and bone. But you are a *person* consisting of spirit, mind, and body, all working together as a unified whole.

This woman perceived her entire being made whole by touching Jesus' clothes. This was her cause, her dream, her goal. And this is why Jesus had come; He was within her reach when she came to touch Him.

5. *She used a point of contact to release her faith.*

This woman made contact with Jesus by touching the hem of His garment. There was no healing power in His clothes themselves, for He said to her, **Thy faith hath made thee whole** (Mark 5:34) — not the touching of His garments. But He did not rebuke her for touching

His clothes because she felt that by so doing she could believe.

Sometimes people find that touching a prayer cloth or putting one upon their bodies helps them release their faith. The power resides in the faith that is released to God. The Lord will honor any point of contact that will help release faith.

As she made her way through the crowd, this woman was saying to herself, "If only I can touch His clothes; if only I can touch His clothes!" Her faith cleared a path for her feet and made an opening through the crowd for her. The people were pressed so closely together that the only way she got through was by faith.

Faith will move God and man; it will take you through when everything else fails. The crowd moved back for this woman to pass as she pressed through, and then...there He was! She had made it to Him. She bent low, reached out a trembling hand, and touched the hem of His robe. It was like touching a live electrical wire.

The mighty healing power of Christ surged into her. It went all through every fiber of her being and fought with her affliction. In a moment she felt that she had been healed: not just her body, but her whole self.

Hundreds of people thronged around Jesus, but this woman was the only one who made contact with the power of God. Jesus turned around and asked, **Who touched me?** (Luke 8:45a).

Peter said, "Lord, what do You mean? The whole crowd is jostling up against You."

"Yes, but this was a different touch," Jesus indicated. "I felt healing power go out of Me." (vv. 45b,46.)

Oh friend, believe it. Jesus is full of healing! He is charged with the mighty power of God to make you completely whole.

This woman's touch was different! She touched the Lord, not as a part of the crowd, but as an individual. She touched Him knowingly, believingly, purposefully. She touched His clothes with a specific purpose; the moment she came in contact with His robe, she believed she received her healing.

This is the way to use a point of contact. The virtue of Jesus heals on contact, bringing deliverance from disease, fear, and frustration. This woman had set the terms for her healing when she said that if she could but touch the hem of His garment she would be made whole. And it happened. It would have taken place had she used some other point of contact, as long as she had believed, then and there.

This is the thing you must grasp and understand! There is more than one possible point of contact, for God cannot be limited to any special thing or person. The simple use of a point of contact is to help us connect with the healing virtue of Jesus.

In Acts 19:11,12 (NIV) we read:

> **God did extraordinary miracles through Paul.**
>
> **Handkerchiefs and aprons that had touched him were taken to the sick, and their illnesses were cured and the evil spirits left them.**

These handkerchiefs and aprons were used as a point of contact. The people knew the items had been in contact with Paul, a great man of God. The moment the articles were placed upon the afflicted, they put their faith in the Lord, and He healed them.

6. She made contact with healing power from God.

This woman felt in her body that she was healed of her illness. Contact was made between her faith and the healing virtue resident in the Person of Jesus Christ.

Just as plugging into an electrical socket makes instant connection with the powerhouse, so faith put into action makes contact with God and releases His power. This limitless power healed the woman of her disease.

7. God's power made her whole.

When Jesus asked, "Who touched Me?" the woman saw that she could not hide, so she came trembling before Him. She told Him why she had touched Him and how she had been healed. Jesus said to her, **...Daughter, be of good comfort: thy faith hath made thee whole; go in peace** (Luke 8:48).

The woman received even more than she had hoped for. She had felt that her need was physical healing. But the Lord gave her what her entire inner being had been crying out for — peace. By connecting peace with healing, Jesus is saying: "You sought healing for your body. But healing is much more than a physical work. Healing is also a spiritual work. Wholeness is a healing for the soul, mind, and body. Your faith has made you completely *whole*."

Let us remember this truth: healing from God is both physical and spiritual. Suppose the woman had received physical healing alone? She would have had health for her body, but not the peace of God in her soul. But when she looked to Jesus for healing, her mind became centered on Him. When she touched His clothes, she was filled with His power and made whole — body and soul.

This woman sent her faith to God, and so can you. God is good and will reward your faith with deliverance.

In Conclusion

1. When you come to the end of yourself, *stop* — before you go to pieces.

2. Believe the story of deliverance and that it is for you.

3. Make a faith-image of Jesus and of being healed by Him.

4. Remember that life is a whole and that Christ seeks to give you life in abundance. Think in those terms and present your *specific* needs to Him.

5. Use a point of contact to touch God. Your faith will lift you out of the crowd.

6. Make contact with Christ's healing power by directing your faith towards Him. He heals on contact.

7. Remember that as a result of your faith, God will make you whole. God rewards those who have faith, and your faith in Him will make you a whole person again.

7

The Paralyzed Man:
Faith Brings Forgiveness
and Freedom

When Jesus saw their faith, he said, "Friend, your sins are forgiven."

..."I tell you, get up, take your mat, and go home."

Luke 5:20,24 NIV

In Luke's account of the healing of the paralyzed man (Luke 5:17-26), we are given one of the most remarkable examples of wholeness in the New Testament. Two things stand out in the story of this man's deliverance: 1) his own need of physical healing, and 2) the presence of the Lord to heal him. God's power to heal is always present when anyone is sick or afflicted.

God loves us, is near us, and wants to heal us. But His healing power is released by faith, and faith alone — active faith that forges ahead in spite of every hindrance, faith that sometimes has to "raise the roof" (v. 19) to get the victory. Healing does not come except as we meet it in the Bible.

With severe paralysis, shut in to himself, and shut out from the world of normal, healthy people, this man was a victim of the tormenting, enslaving power of the devil. God did not place this disease upon him, nor was God receiving any glory from its terrible effect upon his life and home.

The Healing Ministry of Jesus

Jesus came to this earth to bring life. He came not to afflict, but to heal; not to destroy, but to save; not to impoverish, but to enrich; not to drag down, but to lift up; not to send to hell, but to take to heaven. (John 3:16,17; 10:10.)

Jesus Christ came as a Healer, Deliverer, and Lifesaver. Satan is a destroyer and oppressor. Don't blame God for your hurts and ills; He does not send evil, but good: **Every good gift and every perfect gift is from above, and cometh down from the Father of lights, with whom is no variableness, neither shadow of turning** (James 1:17).

In this story of the paralyzed man, Jesus had just returned to Capernaum. He was staying in a house which already was crowded with people who had heard He was there. They had come from every quarter of the land to see and hear the mighty things of God. Even the Pharisees and doctors of the law were present. So great was the multitude in attendance that there was no room for anyone else, even in the doorway. (Mark 2:1,2.)

Luke adds, **...and the power of the Lord was present to heal...**(Luke 5:17). Wherever Jesus is, the power of the Lord is present to heal. This is God's provision for our deliverance from the oppression of the devil. Jesus was, and still is, concerned with the needs of suffering humanity. He wants to set us free, and will do so when we believe in Him and release our faith.

Jesus was always ready to heal and set at liberty those under Satan's oppression. (Luke 4:18,19.) Whenever the captives could get to Him, they found deliverance. Those who came to Him believed in Him for the healing of soul, spirit, and body. Too long have we separated all but our spiritual needs from Christ's atoning work at Calvary. We have spiritualized the Gospel so that it has been applied to the soul, but no longer to the body. However, all the teachings of Jesus related to the *whole* being of man — soul, mind, and body.

As the Savior delivered all who came to Him then, so will He meet all our needs today through His mighty power. The power of God to heal is present today, and whenever and wherever believers will exercise faith, they may benefit from that power.

Not only are believers given the assurance of having their own needs met, but are commanded to **...lay hands on the sick, and they shall recover** (Mark 16:18.) Thus, as disciples of Christ, healing is not only our privilege, it is also our responsibility.

As believers, we are vested with power to heal the sick, cast out devils, and bring deliverance, by faith, to those bound by Satan. (Mark 16:15-18; Matt. 10:1; James 5:15,16.) The Apostle James tells us, **...pray for one another, that ye may be healed...**(James 5:16). We have the responsibility to assist — in a personal, brotherly manner — those suffering under the devil's oppression, and to bring healing to one another.

Four Friends of Faith

Four men in Capernaum took pity on a paralyzed man and resolved to take him to Jesus for deliverance.

Compassion springs from divine love and is more than mere human sympathy. True compassion is identification with another person in his suffering until it is felt that something must be *done* to get him delivered.

These four men took this man's case into their own hands, carrying him bodily to Jesus, since by himself he could not attend the healing service in Capernaum. Before the four took up the corners of the mattress upon which lay the helpless paralytic, they pledged themselves to bold, direct action. Their aim was deliverance, whatever the cost.

Jesus had been in their city before, and His compassionate deliverance of all who came to Him for help had convinced them that He would turn no one away. Confident that if they could get their afflicted friend to Jesus, he would return home completely whole, they began to make their way through the crowd.

This is the goal of every intercessor. Determine in your heart and mind that Christ must be reached. Know that you will reach Him as you press your way through the crowd. Remember: **...he that cometh to God must believe that he is, and that he is a rewarder of them that diligently seek him** (Heb. 11:6).

When they arrived with their charge, the four men of faith and compassion found the way to Jesus blocked by the press of people. As they tried to advance, they were pushed back. They kept trying, but each time the human blockade turned them away. There was just no opening in the crowd. Must they return home defeated? In faith, they refused to give up.

Here is the secret of deliverance. Healing is for those who do not forsake their bold, determined efforts to be healed, those who will not turn back. Julius Caesar, having determined to conquer Britain, sailed with his legions from France to England. Then he burned every ship used for crossing the English Channel. The message was clear: it was either conquer or die! There could be no retreat! Many more could be healed today if they would not give up when the way is temporarily blocked.

How many times the four men tried to get their ailing friend to Jesus we do not know. One thing was fixed in their minds; they would not turn back! When all available means of getting to Jesus failed, these men of determination threw caution to the wind and resorted to drastic action. Daring to go beyond the conventional, tossing aside pride and timidity, these men turned away from the crowd with a divinely conceived plan. With boldness and initiative, they climbed to the top of the house and began tearing off the roof.

This is the kind of people I want to be identified with — the "roof-raisers"! It is time for us, too, to raise the roof for our needs, and get in where the Lord's power is present to heal.

These men were "partners for deliverance." They felt they had a task to do — get their suffering friend healed. There should be a sense of purpose in the heart of every Christian. The purpose of Jesus was to deliver humanity; as His followers, should we not have a similar goal?

God has promised victory to those who seek deliverance. Jesus has assured us: **...where two or three** are gathered together in my name, there am I in the midst of them** (Matt. 18:20). And remember that wherever the Lord is, His power is present to heal.

The Lord's Response to Faith

There are those today who are alarmed at any demonstration of faith to reach Christ for healing, but since God specializes in the impossible and delights in providing redemption for those who demonstrate indomitable faith, we have a perfect scriptural right to make strenuous efforts to receive divine help.

Jesus was never alarmed by any demonstration of faith for deliverance. He was not alarmed that while He was preaching to the people inside the house, there was a commotion above as the four men tore off the tile roof to lower their friend sick of the palsy into His presence.

Jesus was there **...to preach the gospel to the poor;...to heal the brokenhearted,...to preach deliverance to the captives, and recovering of sight to the blind, to set at liberty them that are bruised** (Luke 4:18). When the opportunity came for deliverance, Jesus always went into action, setting the captives free. He preached to build faith, for **...faith cometh by hearing, and hearing by the word of God** (Rom. 10:17). Whenever Jesus saw faith demonstrated, He stopped whatever He was doing and responded to it.

Thank God, we are seeing this same thing today. We should never be so tied to convention, to human plans, to a set pattern, that we will not stop everything — any time — to bring deliverance to the souls and bodies of those in need.

Looking up through the opening in the roof, the Master saw a bed being lowered by four pairs of strong hands. Then He saw something else, something He always looks for before He moves into action. Luke says that He saw **their faith** (Luke 5:20).

The faith of these four men had initiated this scene. Having set as their goal deliverance at any cost, they had burned every bridge. Now, after tearing off the roof, they presented the patient to Christ the Healer.

In faith lies the victory! Thousands of people will never find deliverance unless we manifest faith on their behalf. Believing with others for deliverance is not only our privilege, but also our responsibility.

The faith partners had done all they could. They had completed their faith mission. The roof had been raised, they had made an opening large enough to get their friend through to Jesus, and the paralyzed man was where the power of the Lord was present to heal. Now it was up to the paralyzed man.

There is a time and a place where you are to act on your own. When you get where the Lord's healing power is, you must believe. You must act. *You* too must become a "roof-raiser."

Faith Demands Action

Jesus said to the paralyzed man, **...Arise, and take up thy couch, and go into thine house** (Luke 5:24). It was now time for the sick man to have personal faith, to set his own goal, to break every connection with his affliction, and to actually believe for his deliverance. Others had told him of the Master, others had brought him to the healing service, others had raised the roof for victory, others had brought him where the healing presence of Christ was — but that was not enough.

There is no magic connected with healing. Jesus told the captive to *do* something. When he did what he was commanded by the Lord, then his healing came.

Others can help you release your faith. Then you must put it into action yourself. Faith accomplishes its mission only as it is released. You can have strong faith only as you exercise it. If you were to place a perfectly normal arm in a sling and keep it there in a state of inaction for several months, it would become stiff and useless. So it is with faith. You may have faith lying dormant in your soul, but it will bring deliverance only as you put it to use.

This man had been confined to bed for a long time. His limbs were incapable of lifting and supporting his body. But he had to sever all connections with past defeats, with present afflictions, and with hopes of future freedom. His faith had to be put into action.

Jesus was saying to him: "Arise! Arise in the inner man first, then take up your bed and walk." The inner man standing up helps the outer man to receive new strength into the body. Without hesitation, the man recognized the authority of Jesus over his affliction, and without questioning the Lord's command, he made a gallant effort to rise. To the astonishment of the crowd, he rose up before them, picked up his bed, and departed to his own house, glorifying God.

There are no bonds that faith cannot break, no fetters it cannot sever, no dungeon it cannot open, no disease it cannot heal, no victory it cannot win. Faith puts us directly into the hands of a limitless God Who

...is able to do exceeding abundantly above all that we ask or think, according to the power that worketh in us (Eph. 3:20).

Suffering one, don't try to believe tomorrow or next week or some time in the distant future — believe now! There was a certain moment when Jesus offered this man the miracle of healing: that was the moment when He told him to arise. The secret of deliverance is instant obedience.

When the man arose under the mighty power of God, it penetrated every fiber of his body. The crowd moved back to let him through. His destination now was his home. He had been tied to his bed, shut out from the world, alone in his misery. The devil had stolen the bloom of health from him and had kept him bedfast. But now faith had set him free. Picking up his mattress, he walked out the door to go home. As the people saw him go, they praised God and said to each other, **...We have seen strange things to day** (Luke 5:26).

These people were more impressed with this one healing than they were with all the cut-and-dried church services they had ever attended. God was able to get nearer to them then than at any other time in their lives. There is something about God's love, concern, and healing for the captives of Satan that touches the hearts of men and draws them toward God. The Bible says, **...the goodness of God leadeth...to repentance...**(Rom. 2:4).

Raise the Roof for Victory!

There is only one way to reach the world for Christ, today, and that is to tap into this mighty power of deliverance, by faith. We must bring healing to the whole man. The power of God must fall upon us. The power of the Lord must be present for healing and deliverance. The hurts and ills of humanity must find their solution in our prayers of faith.

Dare we ignore those who are suffering in this crucial hour of the world's great need? Shall we just look on while Satan continues his work of human oppression, when the constant aim of Jesus, the apostles, deacons, and missionaries of the early Church was to heal people in soul, mind, and body? Let us raise the roof for victory!

A person cannot be healed physically without receiving a blessing for his soul also. The same Christ Who healed the paralyzed man's physical afflictions also said to him, **...thy sins are forgiven thee** (Luke 5:20). The man went home saved *and* healed. He was made whole.

Place yourself in the position of this man who found complete deliverance! Raise the roof for victory! Deliverance is yours now, by faith in the same Christ Who lives today to meet every human need.

8

Blind Bartimaeus:
Faith Brings Sight

**"Before they call I will answer;
  while they are still speaking I will hear."**

Isaiah 65:24 NIV

Among Christians throughout the ages the issue of faith has always provoked speculation, tending sometimes to unbelief and often to wrong understanding and application of God's Word on the subject. This situation has resulted in confusion and doubt. A good understanding, appreciation, and application of faith will make a great deal of difference in how you face the zero hours of your life.

Faith is recognized as a vital ingredient in the Christian recipe for happiness, joy, and success in the Lord. Your attitude toward faith will determine whether you find fulfillment or frustration in your walk with God.

As a Gospel preacher who has spoken to thousands of people on every area of human endeavor, I emphasize that faith is the moving force that takes God's Word for what it says. This is important! Faith is essential to answered prayer.

How many times a day do you pray? Once, twice, three times? "As many times as possible," you may say. Great! The Bible does not specify how many times a

91

Christian *ought* to pray, but it does recommend unceasing prayer.

Do you pray with folded hands or uplifted arms, standing up or kneeling down, with closed eyes or bowed head? Whatever the physical stance adopted while praying, sincere prayer must be acted upon by faith if it is to be effective.

The Bible teaches that we have two sets of eyes: our physical eyes and the eyes of our soul. The eyes of our soul have been blinded by Satan if we fail to operate by faith. There are many devout, sincere Christians who are seemingly incapable of standing upon the Word of God.

"Is it *really* true?" they ask.

Bible truth stands sure, with deeper foundations than we can ever comprehend. Faith is the bricks and mortar with which we build our relationship with God. It is our glorious hope of eternity — and for the meeting of our needs today. The story of blind Bartimaeus provides considerable food for thought on the subject of faith. Above all, it offers sublime lessons for the Christian walk in faith. Let's take a brief look at this story which is found in Mark 10:46-52.

Bartimaeus Had Faith To Receive

And they came to Jericho: and as he (Jesus) went out of Jericho with his disciples and a great number of people, blind Bartimaeus, the son of Timaeus, sat by the highway side begging.

And when he heard that it was Jesus of Nazareth, he began to cry out, and say, Jesus, thou Son of David, have mercy on me.

> And many charged him that he should hold his peace: but he cried the more a great deal, Thou Son of David, have mercy on me.
>
> And Jesus stood still, and commanded him to be called. And they call the blind man, saying unto him, Be of good comfort, rise; he calleth thee.
>
> And he, casting away his garment, rose, and came to Jesus.
>
> And Jesus answered and said unto him, What wilt thou that I should do unto thee? The blind man said unto him, Lord, that I might receive my sight.
>
> And Jesus said unto him, Go thy way; thy faith hath made thee whole. And immediately he received his sight, and followed Jesus in the way.

Every morning Bartimaeus would beg from the people who passed by. "Help the blind! Help the blind!" he would cry. Once in a while someone would toss a coin to him. Some cruel, hard-hearted people spat on him. Some abused him and laughed him to scorn.

Surely blind Bartimaeus hoped and longed for a change in his degrading circumstances, an answer to his zero-hour need. Do you not think that the more people laughed and ridiculed him, the more his faith grew for a change? I believe so.

Bartimaeus was helpless, blind, and poor, someone to be pitied, or so it seemed. But one day a message had come to him, and he had never forgotten it. Someone had told him about Jesus of Nazareth Who could heal. And Bartimaeus believed the report.

True Christian faith rests on the specific content of belief; it is not vague wishful thinking that takes the place of real understanding. Blind Bartimaeus sincerely believed in the healing power of Jesus Christ and sat quietly listening to each new account of the exploits of Jesus in nearby towns. He thought to himself, "Jesus would never come to a town like Jericho; but if only He would...." And from this multitude of tiny choices, unrelated circumstances, unnoticed influences, he shaped the strength and substance of his faith, in preparation for a desired change in his status.

Bartimaeus believed with all his heart in the works of Jesus Christ: **How God anointed Jesus of Nazareth with the Holy Ghost and with power: who went about doing good, and healing all that were oppressed of the devil; for God was with him** (Acts 10:38). As a result, Bartimaeus had implicit faith in Christ as a *person* and looked forward to receiving his healing through Him.

Although Bartimaeus had never seen Jesus, he believed His works as true: **And being fully persuaded that, what he had promised, he was able also to perform** (Rom. 4:21).

What is our attitude and reaction in regard to faith, **the evidence of things not seen?** (Heb. 11:1.) Blind Bartimaeus acted upon his faith.

On this particular morning as he staggered along in his tattered robe, he heard a crowd of people gathering down the road. He sensed that something important was taking place, although, of course, he could not see a thing.

"What's happening?" he called out. "Who's coming?" he asked anxiously, only to be met with indifference and rejection.

It was all too much for the poor blind beggar. As the crowd was beginning to move past, he reached out in desperation and frenzy and grabbed hold of someone.

"What's going on?" he asked, in overflowing anger and self-pity. As the man pulled away, he barked back at Bartimaeus, "Jesus of Nazareth is passing by."

The drama that followed was to change Bartimaeus' life forever.

"Jesus of Nazareth! That's the great Teacher I have heard about, the One Who can heal!" he may have pondered momentarily. As we have seen, the Bible says that faith comes by hearing, and hearing by the Word of God. (Rom. 10:17). Blind Bartimaeus had heard about Jesus and believed in Him. In the twinkling of an eye his mind recaptured and assembled all known information about Jesus and His ministry. That knowledge was the solid rock on which he stood, **the substance of things hoped for** (Heb. 11:1).

Faith Believes

The faith factor in the Christian walk is delicate and crucial and deserves detailed study until it is clearly understood. This is not only because that without faith it is impossible to please God, but also because God has given to every person a certain measure of faith. (Rom. 12:3.)

It is sad to hear such exclamations as: "I cannot believe that"; "It is impossible"; "God can't do that." Many dejected people, even some Christians, have taken their "measure of faith" and placed it in something other than God. What do the Scriptures say?

It is better to trust in the Lord than to put confidence in man.

It is better to trust in the Lord than to put confidence in princes.

Psalm 118:8,9

The sad state of affairs today is that many people put their trust in human institutions, science, and knowledge, which (as good as these things are) cannot guarantee them happiness, health, success, and abundant and eternal life. Sooner or later everything in human life changes, every material structure and institution comes tumbling down like a pack of cards. But Jesus Christ is the same yesterday, and today, and forever. (Heb. 13:8.)

I have often pondered over Hebrews 11:6 and its words have always hit me with great freshness and power: **...without faith it is impossible to please him....** Conversely, we can assume that *with* faith we *can* please God. Lack of faith puts us out of line with God. It therefore stands to reason that faith places us in direct contact, in perfect tune, with Him. That sounds interesting, doesn't it? Pick up your Bible and read Hebrews 11:6 as you ask, "What is required of the person who comes to God?" The answer is obvious: he must *believe.*

Faith Stands Upon God's Word

In Mark 10:47 we read: **And when he heard that it was Jesus of Nazareth, he began to cry out, and say, Jesus, thou son of David, have mercy on me.**

As you read this verse, you may realize that Bartimaeus was using a term to identify Jesus (**son of David**) which he could not have read in the Scriptures, because he was blind. Therefore he must have heard this truth from a friend. Nevertheless, Jesus *is* the Son

96

of David, and Bartimaeus heard it and believed it. That was sufficient.

If you read his words carefully, you will conclude that even before the arrival of Jesus, Bartimaeus had implicit confidence in the Lord and His power to relieve him of his handicap, to give him victory over his zero hour.

The Word of God assures us that **...whosoever shall call upon the name of the Lord shall be saved** (Rom. 10:13). Are you not sure that Bartimaeus had this thought in mind?

"Jesus, save me!" he shouted, "Jesus, please! Help me! Mercy! Mercy!"

He was crying for exactly the right thing: mercy. Not only did he cry for the right thing, but he cried out at the right time. There was not a minute to lose, every second counted — Jesus of Nazareth was passing by.

Blind Bartimaeus had a precious gift that you and I need to pray for: the ability to deal with a specific thing at the correct time. The presence of believing faith in our life does not permit us to make vague requests of God. Many people have received no apparent answers to their prayers because they have made the mistake of praying nebulous prayers.

In the Scriptures Jesus declares: **...if two of you shall agree on earth as touching any thing that they shall ask, it shall be done for them of my Father which is in heaven** (Matt. 18:19).

Now, with your believing faith in Christ, do the asking, being mindful of exactly what you need, because there is even greater assurance in the Word:

...If thou canst believe, all things are possible to him that believeth (Mark 9:23.)

Then once you have asked, in faith, do as blind Bartimaeus did and hold to the Word of God until you receive that which you have requested.

Faith in God Brings a Miracle

One afternoon in the early years of my ministry, one of my converts and I stopped for a visit at the home of the young woman I was later to marry. We found the place full of her relatives. There was agitation on every face, and many of the women were crying.

"What's going on?" I inquired.

"It's my uncle's baby," Margaret explained, wiping her tears with the back of her hand. "She was ill for several days, and this morning she died. She kept having convulsions, but the local doctors could do nothing to help her. We even made sacrifices at the juju shrine here in our house, but she died anyway."

"Where is the baby now?" I asked anxiously.

"There," Margaret answered, gesturing toward the bedroom. "We have already bathed the body and bought the coffin for her burial."

With feelings of righteous indignation burning within me, I turned to the father of the child.

"The God I serve can bring your baby back to life," I said confidently. "Will you permit me to pray for her?"

Startled, the father agreed, though he himself was not a Christian.

I walked boldly into the next room where the cold, still form of the baby lay on the bed. I ordered everyone out, except my Christian companion, and closed the door. There was tension and expectation as the relatives waited. Several minutes passed. Suddenly the startled family heard the baby sneeze. They rushed into the room to find the infant awake and looking completely normal.

"She is going to be all right," I told the mother, who gathered the child into her arms. "Give her something to eat," I instructed as I walked out.

Margaret was deeply moved by the event and felt shame for her previous mockery of the Gospel. Now she had seen believing faith in Christ Jesus in action.

"Maybe there *is* something to what Benson is preaching after all," she thought.

Your believing faith will affect people close to you and will force them also to take a stand for Jesus. It is crucial that you stand on the Word of God, maintain a position of unfluctuating trust in the Lord, and walk on to victory, always **looking unto Jesus, the author and finisher of our faith** (Heb. 12:2).

The greatest weakness afflicting professing Christians today is a lack of constancy in the Christian race. Bartimaeus did not allow his faith to waver. Jesus never came that way again. The Lord was on His way to Jerusalem to die. Reading between the lines, you find that if Bartimaeus had not met Jesus that day, he might never have received his sight; he might never have received forgiveness. What a startling thought!

Believing Faith in Jesus Christ

Believing faith in Jesus Christ is honored by God the Father. Jesus has promised us, **...Verily, verily, I say** unto you, Whatsoever ye shall ask the Father in my name, he will give it you (John 16:23). The Apostle Paul tells us without one iota of doubt, ...God shall supply all your need according to his riches in glory by Christ Jesus (Phil. 4:19). We should never forget these truths.

The prayer of faith which God honors is seen in all that our Lord Jesus prayed. He prays for us, and with us, to God, and His prayer is always answered because there is agreement between God the Father, God the Son, and God the Holy Spirit.

God does not go against His Word, which tells us, ...there is one God, and one mediator between God and men, the man Christ Jesus (1 Tim. 2:5). The Bible speaks of the priesthood of Jesus in Hebrews 4:14-16 when it states:

> Seeing then that we have a great high priest, that is passed into the heavens, Jesus the Son of God, let us hold fast our profession.
>
> For we have not an high priest which cannot be touched with the feeling of our infirmities; but was in all points tempted like as we are, yet without sin.
>
> Let us therefore come boldly unto the throne of grace, that we may obtain mercy, and find grace to help in time of need.

God cares about us and our needs more than we can imagine. And in order to meet those needs He asks of us just one thing — believing faith in His Son, the Lord Jesus Christ.

Faith Brings a Life of Fulfillment

Bartimaeus cried out to Jesus, and there was an immediate response. Jesus ...commanded him to be called...(Mark 10:49).

But did blind Bartimaeus feel scared of Jesus and run away in the opposite direction? No. **...casting away his garment,** he rose and came to Jesus as quickly as possible. (v. 50.)

Beloved, walking in faith with God through Jesus Christ demands that we lay aside all else, **...every weight, and the sin which doth so easily beset us...** so that we may freely **...run with patience the race that is set before us** (Heb. 12:1).

Bartimaeus ran to Jesus, and the Lord said to him, **Your faith has made you whole.** (Mark 10:52.) Notice, not "your intellectual understanding," not "your money," not "your works," but "your faith." Faith! That's all it takes.

With a heart overflowing with the blessings of God, I share with you this timeless verse of Scripture written by the Apostle Paul: **I am crucified with Christ: nevertheless I live; yet not I, but Christ liveth in me: and the life which I now live in the flesh I live by the faith of the Son of God, who loved me, and gave himself for me** (Gal. 2:20).

The Bible says that the "just shall live by faith." (Hab. 2:4; Rom. 1:17; Gal. 3:11; Heb. 10:38.) Conversion is really only the beginning of a long pilgrimage, a lifelong journey characterized by high mountain peaks, deep valleys — even some swamps. But, praise God, our unshakeable confidence day by day is that, from the fall of a raindrop to the fall of an empire, all is under the providential hand of God.

God desires for you to live in health, peace, righteousness, freedom, joy, success, and abundance. That is His plan for your life. Put your faith in Jesus

Christ and don't give up. You can have faith to change your business, your home, and your destiny.

Give Jesus Christ a chance. Put all your faith in Him. Walk in Him, and with Him, and you will not only overcome every zero hour in your life, but you will also glimpse a new horizon of unparalleled joy, peace, and victory.

9

Joseph:
Faith Brings Protection
and Promotion

**"...whatever you ask for in prayer, believe that
you have received it, and it will be yours."**

Mark 11:24 NIV

Faith is a fascinating topic for discussion, although
it defies precise definition. In this part of the book, I
intend to bring out the basic elements in faith than can
effect a change in your life.

Faith in God, through Jesus Christ, produces the
same overwhelming results among people of any
nationality, race, or calling. I urge you, therefore, to
cleanse your mind of any wrong teaching that claims
that faith is more effective in certain lands than
elsewhere. That is the devil's lie! I have seen the Bible
work in my life, as in the lives of many others, and I
assure you today that a similar change can come to you
as you act on God's Word of faith.

Faith can change your destiny! The common
denominator among great men and women of God,
servants of the Lord, who have seen lasting changes
in their lives, has always been *faith* in God. This fact
is evident from many biographies and autobiographies
of the great men and women of God. The story of

Smith Wigglesworth, for example, leaves no doubt that faith can change a person's destiny.

Lifted to Higher Ground

Smith Wigglesworth was a plumber. But he believed with all his heart that he should obey Jesus' instruction in Mark 11:22, **...Have faith in God.** He accepted the call of God upon his life — and a new man emerged. The result of his calling to higher ground was the salvation and deliverance of multiplied thousands of people.

My friend, faith in God lifts you to higher ground wherever you may be and whatever God calls you to do. Faith in God to change your destiny always works for the good for all concerned.

The story of Benin City, Nigeria, has been told many times. Now that the city is prosperous, many have forgotten what it used to represent. To call it dreadful would be an understatement. Suffice it to say, it was an unlikely place for God, by man's calculations, to manifest Himself in signs, miracles, and wonders. God looked for a man of faith, a man who would act for Him in faith and help to overthrow the powers of darkness.

I never imagined it could be me as every morning I pinned my tie, put on my well-pressed trousers, and laced my shining shoes. My executive position at the Bata Shoe Company held great prospects for me. I was popular with the management and was confident that, with hard work and perseverance, I could make a great success. I was sure that "the world was my oyster."

Gradually it dawned on me that the tempo of my ministry was increasing. A decision had to be made. Life is full of choices, but faith in God will affect them all, for Christ can do all things. I knew that I was at a crossroads. I had either to hold to to my promising career as a Bata executive, or to launch out by faith into the Master's vineyard.

Praise the Lord that by His grace I opted to serve Him in full-time ministry. I have never regretted my decision.

Faith and Vision

All through life there are moments when you are called to lift up your faith to God through Christ. If you do so, you will never be ashamed. Faith can see you through every zero hour and change your destiny. The vision God gives you will keep you moving forward. Think about this. I believe it takes faith to bring a vision to fruition. Faith and vision are linked.

God's plan for Joseph gives us a clue as to how faith can see a person through his zero hour and change his destiny. Joseph's life is a puzzle, full of lessons about the movement of the hand of God upon the life of a man destined to greatness. It tells of a young man who refused to die before the vision God had given him became a reality.

> Joseph had a dream, and when he told it to his brothers, they hated him all the more. He said to them, "Listen to this dream I had: We were binding sheaves of grain out in the field when suddenly my sheaf rose and stood upright, while your sheaves gathered around mine and bowed down to it."
>
> His brothers said to him, "Do you actually intend to reign over us? Will you actually rule us?" And they

hated him all the more because of his dream and what he had said.

Then he had another dream, and he told it to his brothers. "Listen," he said, "I had another dream, and this time the sun and moon and eleven stars were bowing down to me."

When he told his father as well as his brothers, his father rebuked him and said, "What is this dream you had? Will your mother and I and your brothers actually come and bow down to the ground before you?" His brothers were jealous of him, but his father kept the matter in mind.

Genesis 37:5-11 NIV

God had a great plan for Joseph, hidden in the distant future. Joseph could not forget those impressive dreams of the glorious future which God had scheduled in His timetable. Yet when he told his father and brothers about them, they were resentful of the drama. Imagine how Joseph must have spent time musing on his dreams. Humanly speaking, he did not know how God was going to bring His great promises to pass, but he had faith that somehow they would be fulfilled.

God Is in Control

So when Joseph came to his brothers, they stripped him of his robe — the richly ornamented robe he was wearing — and they took him and threw him into the cistern. Now the cistern was empty; there was no water in it.

As they sat down to eat their meal, they looked up and saw a caravan of Ishmaelites coming from Gilead. Their camels were loaded with spices, balm and myrrh, and they were on their way to take them down to Egypt.

> **Judah said to his brothers, "What will we gain
> if we kill our brother and cover up his blood? Come,
> let's sell him to the Ishmaelites and not lay our hands
> on him...."**
>
> **Genesis 37:23-27** NIV

Sometimes when men become aware of God's
favor upon someone, they plot to destroy God's goal
for that individual; but in almost all cases their schemes
only enhance the Master's plan. Envy, treachery, and
machinations flow from the hearts of men blind with
jealousy as they struggle to abort God's plan for His
servants. But they always fail.

The brothers of Joseph were hell-bent on
destroying him. The Bible tells us that they sold him
to the Ishmaelites who were going to Egypt.

Did the cruelty of Joseph's brothers put God's plan
out of action? Of course not; God was still in control!

Even as a small boy, as he lay there in the muddy
pit, Joseph's faith remained steadfast. If the dream is
from God, and you remain constant in faith, then what
He has said will be fulfilled.

The Ishmaelites bundled Joseph off to Egypt,
having no idea how precious he was to God. Joseph's
tribulations were beginning to gather momentum. Later
we read how he was falsely accused by the wife of his
employer who had him thrown into prison. (Gen. 39.)
"*When* will this dream God showed me come to pass?"
Joseph may have wondered, as he stood, sadly, behind
prison bars.

Your belief that faith can see you through your zero
hour and change your destiny will be tested and tried.
Joseph's faith was tested too, but he kept his eyes on
the glory God had revealed to him. Even the seductive

speech of an enchantress like Potiphar's wife could not throw him off balance. Joseph was determined; he had made up his mind to stand firm and **...the Lord was with him, and that which he did, the Lord made it to prosper** (Gen. 39:23).

God was with Joseph, even in prison: the God Who showed the dream to Joseph did not desert him — because he demonstrated faith regardless of circumstances.

Never Despair

Many believers miss the blessings of God because they allow despair and temporary distractions to water down their faith in God. Just hold on to Him!

Paul gave Timothy the same advice in 2 Timothy 1:12:

> **For the which cause I also suffer these things: nevertheless I am not ashamed: for I know whom I have believed, and am persuaded that he is able to keep that which I have committed unto him against that day.**

Joseph's vision and dream did not diminish just because he was thrown into a pit by his brothers. Likewise, whatever your family, friends, or enemies do to you *must not* affect your faith in God: this is crucial. The fact that Joseph was falsely accused and imprisoned did not distract him from his vision. Joseph's well-grounded faith in God protected him like a suit of armor. Remember, faithful is He Who promises. (Heb. 10:23.)

God fulfilled Joseph's vision. The descriptions of his later years in Egypt make interesting reading. We see him adorned in beautiful, richly embroidered clothes as ruler of the country. Men, women, and children of all backgrounds bow down to him in homage. He exercises power and authority over all Egypt.

Glance back and see him lying helpless in the pit, refusing to die. Take a look at him behind prison bars, trusting God to put things right. Joseph would soon have been dead, buried, and forgotten if he had yielded to doubt, fear, and unbelief. The only reason he came through his zero hour and saw a change in his destiny was because he kept immovable faith in God.

Through the faith and obedience of one man, Joseph, God fulfilled a great vision. It was not only Joseph's destiny that was changed; the vision touched people and generations yet unborn. With good reason he was able to tell his brothers after it was all over: **And God sent me before you to preserve you a posterity in the earth, and to save your lives by a great deliverance** (Gen. 45:7).

Faith can change your destiny, my friend. Stand up and act in positive faith toward God. In the midst of your zero hour, hold on. God will see you through to victory.

10

A Vision Fulfilled

And now these three remain: faith, hope and love....

1 Corinthians 13:13 NIV

Many years ago, very early in my ministry, I heard a man remark, "Without faith, a person's life is filled with dreary failures." It took me some time to appreciate the wisdom in that saying. Faith is a magnetic word for those who understand what it means. Lack of faith results in diverse negative influences. An individual without faith may look at his fellows with downright suspicion and distrust: the basic comfort and assurance of real friendship is lost. Worse still, he may even begin to think that the whole world is against him. Then, gradually, the joy of living begins to wear off.

As a preacher of the Word for almost thirty years, across some eighty countries around the world, I have seen that when men lose faith they lose their great ideals and their sense of purpose. Instead of being filled with positive enthusiasm and expectation, they become obsessed with a sickening "what's-the-use" attitude.

One man defined faith as "continuing to believe in certain truths no matter what happens." Steadfastness is an integral part of the faith walk with God. One of the greatest statements in the Bible is Paul's **...I have kept the faith** (2 Tim. 4:7). He also wrote, **Now**

abideth faith.... (1 Cor. 13:13), meaning that no matter what else happens, faith will last.

A great American preacher has pointed out that the real profanity of man is not the use of a few swear words. The most profane utterance that can pass human lips is the word "hopeless." Whenever we say that a particular situation or person is hopeless, we are slamming the door in the face of God. There is no such thing as a hopeless situation or person. As Christians, we are not to give up; tenacity of purpose yields fruits. All we need to back up our faith in God is a bit of patience and perseverance.

Abiding Faith

Paul's writings to the Corinthians make good reading. My own favorite verse is First Corinthians 13:13: **And now abideth faith, hope, charity, these three....**

The word "abideth" implies remaining consistent. Over the years of preaching the Gospel, I have heard some unbelieving people make the comment, "Faith is a risky business." If that is so, then "blessed assurance" becomes "blessed insurance"! The faith which gives strength and assurance in the zero hours, transforms lives, and brings visible change is one that believes God is working among us and not just watching us from afar.

The Miracle Centre in Benin City, Nigeria, has been documented as one of the largest churches in the world. I have served that church as pastor for many years and have preached on faith there time and time again. On occasion I have been grieved to see some members of the church who are unable to launch out toward God in faith.

112

From time to time I have heard the negative remark, "This situation is hopeless; I feel like giving up."

My frank reply has always been: "Quitters never win, and winners never quit."

If we will be faithful, in time God will reveal His will to us through the workings of divine providence. I know what I am talking about because He has done so in my own life and call to the ministry.

You must get it established in your mind that however God may choose to reveal His will in your life, whatever the particular act He may call upon you to perform, your response must be based on nothing else but faith.

Schweitzer's Choice

Have you ever read about Albert Schweitzer? He is considered by many to be one of the greatest Christians of all time. Surely this wonderful reputation has something to do with his faith in God, which ultimately changed his life and consequently his destiny.

The moment came when Albert Schweitzer had to decide upon the subject of his life's work. That moment comes for every man and woman at least once in a lifetime. Schweitzer was known to be an exceptionally brilliant young man. His problem was that he had so many abilities — in medicine, music, teaching. Today he is considered a master in each of these fields.

Countless opportunities cross our path, but each life-changing decision must be based on faith in God. What should we do? What must be our stand?

Schweitzer faced the same dilemma. One day he was tidying up his desk. Among the discarded papers was a little yellow magazine from the Paris Missionary Society. It was addressed, in fact, to a neighbor, but had been put in Schweitzer's mailbox by mistake. It was all part of God's plan.

Glancing through the brochure, Schweitzer noticed an article entitled, "The Needs of the Congo Mission." Over and over again he read the article and then it began to dawn on him — God was calling him to Africa.

He had easily achieved worldwide distinction in theology and music and had gone on to earn a doctorate in medicine. He had also served as assistant minister in a busy parish and had become a skilled interpreter of the organ music of Bach.

Some people draw a dividing line between faith and intellect, but not Schweitzer, despite all his education. Faith does not suspend our sense of good judgment, it reinforces it. His friends regarded his decision to go and work in Africa as professional suicide. But soon he became more widely known through his work in the Dark Continent than would ever have been the case had he tried to hold on to a wealthy following in any famous clinic or concert hall.

Was it just an accident that the postman put that little magazine in the wrong mailbox? Was it mere chance that it lay unnoticed until the timely moment when Dr. Schweitzer's mind was ready to receive direction?

Many people don't respond to God when they should because they find it hard to discern His involvement in the daily events of life. Open up by faith today and believe that, as the famous hymn writer wrote, "God moves in a mysterious way."

Dr. Schweitzer could have sat comfortably in his office and decided that he would lose too much by going to Africa. Thank God, he did not. He was willing to thrust out in faith to God, and his destiny was changed.

Through faith we know that God has worked out a better purpose for us. If you will only read Hebrews 11, you will know that faith can change your destiny. What was said of the saints of old can also be true of you: **But now they desire a better country, that is, an heavenly: wherefore God is not ashamed to be called their God: for he hath prepared for them a city** (Heb. 11:16).

Faith makes us desire better things from God and for God in accordance with His promise.

Special Words From God

Faith changed my destiny. Today, in response to God's unfolding plan in my life, I have launched out in faith.

God told me, "I, the Lord, will open a door in the United Kingdom for you to preach My name among the English." I believed Him.

Believing God's Word at the moment you read it or the instant it comes into your heart makes a world of difference in your success. Some hear the Word through one ear, and it passes out through the other.

Some take the Word into their hearts and allow it to die in their minds. You need to hear, believe, and act upon the Word of the Lord. Confess it, respect it, hold fast to it, because God says of His Word, **...it shall not return unto me void, but it shall accomplish that which I please, and it shall prosper in the thing whereto I sent it** (Is. 55:11).

It was several years ago, in Benin City, that I heard God's special instruction to me. He woke me up one cold night, and I sat wrapped in my coverings on the side of the bed. As I waited there in silence, I could sense the Spirit of God ministering in my heart about the United Kingdom. As far as I could see, there was no knowing as to how the Lord was going to accomplish the plan He was revealing to me, but nevertheless I believed Him.

I realize that this is where the trouble emerges for many Christians. If you have been called of the Lord, settle the issue in your mind. Move it down into your heart and all will be well.

"Lord," I prayed, "I have no funds to make such a grand outreach to the United Kingdom."

Then God spoke back confidently to me: "I, the Lord Who called you, will open the doors. I will provide the passage, and you will preach My name."

All to myself I shouted an affirmative, "Amen and alleluia!"

It was still dark. The clock by my bed continued to tick obediently. It was 2:00 a.m. Looking over toward my wife, I could see that she was still in deep sleep. Slowly I stretched my body onto the bed and went back to sleep.

But God had not had His last word yet on this United Kingdom outreach. As I slept, I had a dream. There I was in London. Before me were beautiful buildings, carefully mown lawns, and sleek cars. As I walked along the street, I saw thousands upon thousands of people moving in all directions. Suddenly my eyes came to rest on a grand-looking, five-star hotel, and I felt compelled to walk toward it. Within the precincts of this charming place I was met by a handsome-looking man who stretched out his hand familiarly to me.

"Welcome, we have been expecting you," he said.

I was so taken aback by the warm reception and the glamor of the surroundings that I forgot to reply.

Then I followed the man along corridor after corridor, until we stopped in a very spacious and magnificent parlor. I was beckoned to take my seat. Everything there was of the very best. As I settled down, I began to notice something else. The interior decorations of the parlor were all in red. And the room glittered gloriously as the lights came on. The waiters who attended me were in red attire to match their surroundings. It was breathtaking.

"What can we offer you, sir?" the handsome English waiter asked me.

Before I could reply, he gave me a long list of all that was available. I sighed. With care I placed my order, and when it finally arrived I was satisfied with everything.

After the meal, a courteous official appeared, picked up my bag, paid the bill, and ushered me out. I had the full red-carpet treatment.

I pondered over this impressive dream for many days. I could not get it out of my mind.

The years passed by, and I went around the world preaching the Gospel of salvation through Jesus Christ. Invitations swarmed into my office from every continent on the globe. I often had to turn down invitations. My tight schedule at home and abroad was bursting at the seams. I went to Australia, then to the United States. I traveled to the Far East to present the Good News of Jesus to the Malaysians. Europe called, and I answered. I had the privilege of preaching in other African countries and in several places in North America.

One day I looked though my passport and examined the stamps of various countries, collected as I had visited these nations to preach the Gospel. I had been to more than seventy-five countries to proclaim the Risen Christ. Yet that vision and dream of going to the United Kingdom had not been fulfilled. But my faith in God remained as resolute as ever.

Vision Fulfilled

At the end of 1984 I received a letter with a British postmark. It was from the Reverend Wynne Lewis of Kensington Temple in London.

"We have read your book *Fire In His Bones*,"[1] he wrote, "and have heard all that God has been doing through you around the world. Would you be able to come over to Britain in May 1985 and minister to us?"

The United Kingdom had called me at last! "I will come," was my immediate reply.

---

[1](Tulsa: Praise Books, 1981).

I went to London in May 1985, a journey that was to be the fulfillment of a dream and a vision of seven year's standing. A high-powered delegation of Pentecostal leaders welcomed me at Heathrow airport and drove me to a first-class hotel in central London.

"This is a familiar place," I said to myself as the door of the car was flung open for me to get in. The smooth lawn reminded me of a place I had visited before. I tried to think where and when.

Lifting my eyes, I surveyed the immaculate edifice of the hotel as we entered the reception hall. As we walked through the corridors and went up in the elevator, it hit me with renewed intensity: "I have been here before — but when?"

A massive glass door opened before me, as my hosts led the way forward. A shining red carpet heralded our arrival. The walls were laced with exquisite decorations of the finest quality. I stood speechless. A steward arrived, spotlessly dressed. He positioned himself near me and said courteously, "We have been expecting you, sir; what can we offer you?"

In a split second the curtain within my mind was swept back and I recalled my dream and vision. To the most minute detail, the Lord had fulfilled it. It may have taken several years, but time could not change the Master's plan for my life.

Nothing can alter what God has set out to do. My dear friend, if you will only believe in your heart and accept the truth that faith in God can bring your dreams to pass, you will be so much happier.

Through faith, I believe God's Word. Though faith I know He is faithful. Trials and tribulations could not take away Joseph's dream; neither could they erase mine. Faith can see you through your zero hour and change your destiny. I assure you that as you place your faith in Christ, new visions will take shape in your life, some of them far beyond anything you could imagine. Praise the Lord!

11

From Hindsight to Foresight

**...Forgetting what is behind and straining toward
what is ahead, I press on toward the goal to win the
prize for which God has called me heavenward in
Christ Jesus.**

Philippians 3:13,14 NIV

The first step toward a calm confidence in the
future is to learn to believe that life is good. That belief
comes from having faith in a God Who you know holds
the future, as well as your life, in His hands. Ours is
a *big* God, and expressed faith in Him results in big
achievements.

The real trouble with a lot of people is the fact that
their God is too small. They have limited Him. What
did the great Apostle Paul say? **...my God shall supply
all your need...**(Phil. 4:19). What Paul meant was that
he served a big God.

Past, Present, and Future

Many people have no concern about yesterday —
after all, it is gone. Others busy their lives thinking
about past misfortunes; the records show that such
people never get far into the future. Like the proverbial
ostrich, they bury their heads in the sands of the past,
unwilling to look at either the present or the future.

I firmly believe that when our lives are in harmony
with God's will though our faith, we have that

instinctive sense of the right direction, which is the Holy Spirit's guidance, even though we cannot see the way ahead. This is because the Word of God is a lamp unto our feet, and a light unto our path. (Ps. 119:105.)

The journey of life into the future must be traveled one step at a time. The Bible says that God sheds His glorious light on our path. All we need to do is to keep walking forward in trusting confidence and unstained fellowship. As we move steadily and fearlessly ahead, we know that through the storms and unavoidable uncertainties we will come at last to the right place.

My word to you on this subject is this: move on by turning your face toward the dim unknown of tomorrow, believing that every step of the way the hands of the Almighty cover you.

In the Twenty-Third Psalm, David wrote of the Lord: **Yea, though I walk through the valley of the shadow of death, I will fear no evil: for thou art with me...**(v. 4). David knew that there would be valleys ahead. But the word "through" is crucial. You will fear no evil because you know that when you walk *through* it, God will be right there with you.

David also wrote of the Lord, **...for thou art with me....** When your whole life is centered in God, He will be there to see you through the good times and the bad. You know that somehow, through your faith in Him, all things will work out fine.

Faith is mentioned more and more in the New Testament because it is a new-covenant work whose theme is: **The just shall live by faith.** (Rom. 1:17; Gal. 3:11; Heb. 10:38.)

It is sad that thousands of Christians are spending their precious lives believing the devil's lie. On the verge of tears, they will say, "I just can't make it; I have no faith!" They depend upon other people's faith for the miracles they need.

Don't be one of these people. Act upon the Word of God and receive your own miracle! Every Christian has equal rights, and it is God's will and His heart's desire that each one of His children learn how to avail himself of all His blessings. Believe the words you are hearing and reading, act upon them, and see your tiny acorn-seed of faith develop into a giant oak-tree miracle in every area of your life.

Faith That Works

Jesus left behind, for all His followers, the key to God's storehouse:

> And Jesus answering saith unto them, Have faith in God.
>
> For verily I say unto you, That whosoever shall say unto this mountain, Be thou removed, and be thou cast into the sea; and shall not doubt in his heart, but shall believe that those things which he saith shall come to pass; he shall have whatsoever he saith.
>
> Mark 11:22,23

Jesus emphasized **faith in God**. (v. 22.) It should not surprise you to learn that this verse was among the collection I memorized very soon after my conversion. The glamor of it has not been lost through the years. If anything, I have come to appreciate even more the powerful secret of having deep-seated faith in God.

Jesus said that we are to have faith in *God* — not in ourselves, our friends, our faith, occult powers, secret societies, or the mastermind of evil, Satan. The reason the Lord told us to have faith in God is simple: faith in God the Creator works much more effectively than faith in any form of His creation.

The exhortation of Jesus for us to have faith in God is followed by another powerful word of scripture: **For verily I say unto you, That whosoever** [that strictly refers to any person; me as well as you] **shall say unto this mountain... (v. 23). Notice that the faith that is described here is straightforward, specific, and definite.**

I would like to issue a challenge to you at this point. Select any circumstance of your own life in which there is a blockage and apply to it the force of faith. I assure you with all my heart, as a servant of the living God, this "faith formula" will work.

...Be thou removed... (v. 23). These words mean just what they say. The stumbling block or barrier to your dream, vision, or goal, is removed by faith in God.

In the next portion of the scripture which we are exploring, Jesus says that if we will do as He says, then every barrier of faith will be **...cast into the sea....** (v. 23). That is, it will be gone forever. When the hindrance or blockage is gone, complete victory lies in wait.

In Mark 11:23, the two most important words stand face to face with each other — **doubt and believe.** To move forward in faith, you must conquer doubt at all costs, knowing that God is true (Rom. 3:4) and that He will keep His Word regardless of what doubt may say.

God Never Gives Up

I repeat: faith *can* change your destiny. It worked for me in Africa, and it can work for you wherever you are. The same unchangeable God rules and reigns over the whole universe. Any deficiencies are within our faith. But it is impossible to have faith in God without knowledge of His Word.

Now is the time to direct your faith to God and see yourself a master of the crisis, the zero hour, that is rocking you. You may be tempted to give up and cry out, "I can't do it," but that is a defeatist attitude.

God never gives up on anyone — neither must you give up on yourself or on your situation. Paul told us, **Fight the good fight of faith...**(1 Tim. 6:12). Develop your faith. Build upon it. Experience it. Don't allow anyone or anything to spoil the vision God has imbedded in your heart. Believe that God will stand by you, and all will be well.

One thing has seen me through all the zero hours of my life and has brought me through the storms and tough times in my ministry. One thing has made all the difference: faith in God.

Faith can bring you through your zero hours and change your destiny, just as it has done for me. Even as you read these words, I urge you to believe that the power of God is being released in your life. Place your entire faith in Him now!

Making Full Proof of Faith

By the grace of God, I have seen faith work more miracles than most Christians will ever be privileged to witness in their entire lives on this earth. I have seen faith in God work in my family, in the church, and in many other areas of life. Faith has no limits. Faith does not recognize any hindrance. Faith in God based upon the Word overcomes all stumbling blocks. Faith can change your destiny, *if* you will let it. Will you?

My ministry is so full of convincing testimonies to the wonder-working power of faith that today I have no doubt as to what it can do. Truly *all* things are possible with God. (Matt. 19:26.) With faith, even our human disappointments can be turned into His divine appointments.

It may be hard to believe that Paul's confinement in prison was God's appointment. But although Paul saw all that represented the injustice, cruelty, and wickedness of men, he also managed to turn his disappointments into God's appointments. (2 Cor. 11.)

Faith in God changes things, no matter how hopeless they may look. Paul followed his own advice to others, and **having done all,** he was able **to stand.** (Eph. 6:13.) By turning to God for inspiration and aspiration, he turned his excuses to uses. These are the ingredients of faith.

Paul had dreamed of going one day to Spain. Instead, he ended up in a Roman prison! Some would have merely folded their hands, done nothing, and wasted away. Others would have cried out to heaven or would have accused God to His face, as Job's unthoughtful wife advised him to do. (Job 2:9.) Paul knew better. He tenaciously dedicated himself to God, even in prison. Later he wrote, **But I would ye should understand, brethren, that the things which happened unto me have fallen out rather unto the furtherance of the gospel** (Phil. 1:12). Paul knew that although he could not get through to the multitudes in Spain, he *could* win the guards in prison.

We can learn a lesson from Paul's experience: "If you cannot have the opportunities you grasp, then grasp the opportunities you have." Paul's prison epistles contain some of his deepest revelations from the treasures of God's wisdom and knowledge.

Faith changed the destiny of Paul. Faith can change your destiny also.

Coping With "Failure"

It may well be that, like Paul, you have missed out on something you dreamed of. Perhaps you have ended up in a position of disappointment. Now, if you can't escape your prison, let God help you make something out of it. Disappointments, failures, and trials are the eggs we break to make the omelettes of life's success. If only you will give God a chance, disappointments can become the stepping-stones to great achievements.

I have shown you how the Apostle Paul recognized this forceful fact. He said boldly, **...forgetting those things which are behind, and reaching forth unto those things which are before** (Phil. 3:13). If only you will understand that just as faith overcomes fear, and love conquers hate, so positive action surmounts past failures. Stop keeping company with your failures. Lift high your head, look into tomorrow, and let the sky be your limit.

Prayer

Prayer to God, from the point of view of a born-again Christian, is a definite act of faith. Expecting an answer to prayer is an act of faith. Acting on the revelation of God to bring to pass His will is an act of faith. This is the faith which alters situations. This is the faith which changes the destiny of men and women through Jesus Christ our Lord.

I don't understand prayer any more than I understand electricity. But I do know that the mysterious power of electricity can be harnessed to do many useful things. Likewise consistent prayer increases faith, while a lack of prayer is harmful: "Seven days without prayer makes one weak!" Prayer is a propeller to faith. It rises up and moves forward to its destination.

Unceasingly, people thronged to Jesus to hear Him preach, listen to Him teach, and see Him heal. One day a man came to Christ seeking urgent help for his sick son. Jesus was ready. The man said to Him, **...if thou canst do any thing, have compassion on us, and help us** (Mark 9:22). Do you see where he put the "if"? "If *thou* canst do anything," he said. The "if" of man is in reference to Christ. But the Lord calmly corrected that statement by replying, **...If *thou canst believe*, all things are possible to him that believeth** (Mark 9:23).

Better get it clear that the "if" is not with God; it is with us! Jesus said plainly that the only limit to our prayer is the limit of our own belief — the mental actualization of the vision which is in the mind.

Before a building is built, the architects draw up the plans for it. And, to paraphrase Edison, "Anything the mind of man can conceive, the hand of man can construct." Similarly, anything the heart of man can believe, faith in God can create.

Believing is drawing up a mental blueprint. When that plan is firmly settled in the mind, the word "impossible" is eliminated from the thinking. If science says that it can conceive and build, then faith declares that it can believe and create.

In the course of my travels around the world, I have seen some of the most magnificent buildings ever designed and constructed by man. Sometimes I look at the grandeur, finesse, and elegance of these fabulous works of architecture and say to myself, "Lord, give me a vision of these great edifices for the expansion of Your Kingdom in Africa."

Those who have no faith think that God does not answer prayer, but as a man of faith I know He does. Today, in Benin City, Nigeria, there stands a magnificent edifice which was once only a dream in my heart and mind. That dream became reality because I acted upon it in faith, trusting my God to bring to pass that which He had revealed to me through His Word.

You can do the same with your dream. Don't lose sight of your vision. Faith makes all things possible. Faith can change your situation, circumstance, and destiny, if only you will believe God's Word and act upon it.

Conclusion

In this book, I have attempted to set forth some of the spiritual truths which I have discovered in a lifelong tested and proven faith walk with God. Renew your mind with these lessons and you will never be the same again. Not even the devil can hold you back.

Life is similar to mountain climbing in that the climber is always struggling higher and higher. But it is different in that in life we never reach the top. We never arrive because we never run out of heights to scale. But go out and aim for life's highest point, because faith in God can see you through your zero hour and change your destiny!

The Harrison House Vision

Proclaiming the truth and the power
Of the Gospel of Jesus Christ
With excellence;

Challenging Christians to
Live victoriously,
Grow spiritually,
Know God intimately.

Dr. **Benson Idahosa,** Archbishop and founder of Church of God Mission International in Benin City, Nigeria, has established 5,000 churches throughout Nigeria and Ghana since 1971. Many of the ministers he supervises pastor churches of 1,000 to 4,000 people. He is president of Faith Medical Centre, a government approved hospital.

Soulwinning is Dr. Idahosa's primary concern. With a motto of "Evangelism, Our Supreme Task," he works toward his goal of reaching the state capitals of Nigeria as well as the other nations of Africa with the Gospel of the Lord Jesus Christ. A black African, he finds the doors of the nations of Africa wide open to him. Already, he has ministered in over 101 countries.

With crusades playing an important part in his ministry, Dr. Idahosa is involved in at least one crusade per month. Record crowds of nearly one million people nightly attended the Lagos crusade in April, 1985.

Dr. Idahosa established The Redemption TV ministry. With a potential viewing audience of 50 million people, the program will deeply impact the Moslem territories.

Dr. Idahosa holds a Diploma of Divinity from Christ for the Nations Institute in Dallas, Texas, which he attended in 1971, a Doctor of Divinity degree, received in 1981 from the Word of Faith College in New Orleans, and a Doctor of Laws degree from Oral Roberts University in March, 1984. He also holds various degrees from the International University in Brussels, Belgium.

In addition to filling the position of Archbishop of Church of God Mission International, Inc., Dr. Idahosa is also chairman of the Board of Trustees of that church, a member of the College of Bishops of the International Communion of Christian Churches, and President of All Nations for Christ Bible Institute.

Dr. Idahosa and his wife, Dr. Margaret Idahosa, have four children.

Additional copies of
Strangers to Failure — Developing Faith and Power in an Awesome God
are available from your local bookstore or from:
💷 Harrison House • P. O. Box 35035 • Tulsa, OK 74153

To contact the author, write: Archbishop Benson Idahosa
P. O. Box 29400 • Washington, D.C. 20017